The Autobiography of a Working Woman

Adelheid Popp

THE
AUTOBIOGRAPHY OF
A WORKING WOMAN

BY

ADELHEID POPP

439-268

ᴛᴀᴏ

TRANSLATED

By E. C. HARVEY

WITH INTRODUCTION TO AMERICAN EDITION BY JENKIN
LLOYD JONES, LINCOLN CENTER, CHICAGO

AND INTRODUCTIONS TO ENGLISH EDITION BY AUGUST
BEBEL AND J. RAMSAY MACDONALD, M.P.

CHICAGO
F. G. BROWNE & CO.
LONDON: T. FISHER UNWIN
1913

331.4

THE AUTOBIOGRAPHY OF A
WORKING WOMAN

INTRODUCTION

"ADELHEID POPP" is a name that has a far-away sound, and a superficial reading of this "Autobiography of a Working Woman" may confirm the sense of remoteness. Vienna is far away from America. The conditions of a working woman there are necessarily somewhat different from those of a working woman in New York or Chicago. The conditions of the latter may be somewhat less dismal, but the differences are superficial, the similarities are profound.

We rejoice in the appearance of an American edition of this marvelous autobiography, which, judged from a literary standpoint, has the freshness, power, and originality that characterize genius. The very simplicity, directness, frankness, and insight, prove the unconscious, and on that account unpretentious, power of this unsophisticated woman, which broke through her illiteracy and thwarting obstacles by the power of suffering and disinterested service.

Here is the story of a "working woman" who has felt the bitterness of hard, unrelenting toil, and out of the agony of such a life has been brought into sympathy with the Gospel side of co-operation. By bitter tears her eyes were cleared to read the illuminating message *of the great democratic movement that assumes the name "socialism" in many quarters.*

That working men and women will read this book with bated breath and tearful sympathy, goes without the saying. But it is a book for the employer more than for the employee, for the more favored rather than the less favored. It is a book that ought to find a place among the religious books on the center-table of the rich.

In America, as in Austria, the anxieties of the unemployed are more pitiful than the most relentless grind of the employed. Here as there, awful temptations and persistent dangers beset the unbefriended, the underfed, and the suppressed life of a working girl. The purity of womanhood is menaced almost everywhere where shop and factory toil obtains under unsanitary and over-exacting conditions. But these heart-breaking conditions and dangers are not so gruesome as those which surround weary feet in their futile search for any toil, however humble, that will bring any wage, however unworthy. To read this book is to realize that there is one thing worse, even for children, than hard work, and that is enforced idleness, bordering on starvation. They who will not work, perhaps deserve little pity, let them go hungry; but they who would work but starve in the ranks of the unemployed, or are pushed into the more deplorable ranks of those who must feed themselves by crime, lay the darkest charge that can be brought against present economic conditions, the brutalities of the modern industrial world.

This book is to be commended to those who think that socialism is primarily, or chiefly, an economic dream carrying with it some kind of irreligious recoil from the established order of things. To the mind of this writer, the word socialism has carried with it in some quarters certain crass conceptions of soul, certain theological or non-theological dogmas concerning the origin, nature, and destiny of life, certain crude and, for the present at least, impracticable, perhaps almost impossible, programs concerning the distribution of wealth. But socialism also represents increasingly a profound search for economic justice, a hunger for civic and social righteousness. It is a sincere attempt to render the Gospel of Jesus in terms of industrial fair play. It represents a passion for service, it carries with it, oftentimes, a self-denying enthusiasm for the multitude, a zeal for brotherhood, a practical piety that appeals with increasing power to the unbiased student.

Incidentally, this little handbook in sociology, for it deserves this unassumed title, throws light upon the hideous monster, militarism — the wicked waste of time, strength, and money devoted to the idle and worse than useless industries of destruction, the instruments of hate, the guardians and promoters of class distinctions.

The story of this gifted working girl would be heart-breaking were it not shot through and through with a purity unsullied, with a fine, unsatisfied hunger of an intellect ever growing, of a sweet maidenhood blooming at last into a passion for humanity.

Let it be read by the complacent "leisure class" who are so busy and often over-worked with secondary interests and unnecessary industries, that they may have some glimpse of the life that they are losing, discover perchance some glimpse of a joy not theirs but within their reach — the joy of self-sacrifice.

No one reading this book can fail to see that it is a contribution to the religious life of the individual life as well as the community and the age. There is something sacramental in the confession the author makes when she tells us that on the day she went for the weekly newspaper, the organ of the Social Democrats, which she was to distribute, she put on her best dress, "as I used to do when I went to Church." She reaches far down towards the roots of the spiritual life when she tells us that on the very evening of the day that she had argued with her fellow workers that there could not be an omnipotent God, because if there were, so many men would not have to suffer such hardships in their lives, "I folded my hands as I lay in bed and raised my eyes to the image of the Madonna, and I again involuntarily thought. 'Still it may perhaps be true.'" Her testimony is worth something when she says: "Socialism has lent my life so much peace that I have strength to go through much without succumbing." Hers was the insatiable hunger of an intellect that "read without choice whatever came to hand," reaching the devout climax, the synthesis of the saint, when she says: "To be inspired to serve a great cause gives so much joy and lends such high worth to life that one can bear very much without losing courage. I learned to acknowledge that in my own experience."

It is to be hoped that this book, now made available to American readers, will help many, more favored than this working girl, to a vision of the same truth and to the peace of a similar experience.

JENKIN LLOYD JONES

\BRAHAM LINCOLN CENTER, CHICAGO,
January 11, 1913.

ADELHEID POPP.

MARGARET MACDONALD, 1900, WITH HER CHILD, ALISTER.

To face p. 5

INTRODUCTION TO THE
ENGLISH EDITION

ONE of the last acts of my wife's life was
to arrange with Mr Unwin for the publica-
tion of this book. She had come across it
in its original German; she knew Frau Popp,
whose hard life it unveils, and I well remember
how both the story and the woman captivated
her. She was to have written this introduction, but that was one of her many projects
that will have to be carried out by others
or remain altogether undone. She was in
correspondence with Frau Popp when she
died, and some of the material which I shall
use came to her after her eyes were closed
for ever and her heart could respond no more
to earthly things. If it be that she still
follows our interests, I know nothing will
please her more than that this tale of the
struggle of her friend should be given to
English readers, associated with her name
and memory.

She, like the rest of us Socialists, had

a passion for international friendship, and
one of her most cherished dreams was to
bring the Socialist women of this country
into fraternal and vital touch with the Continental women. No jaunt filled her with more
child-like joy than the jaunts to Amsterdam,
to Stuttgart, and to Copenhagen, where the
International Congresses of Socialism have
been held recently, and at these Congresses
no one worked more strenuously than she did
to establish a communion of mind between
the Continental women and our own. At
one of these Congresses she met Frau Popp,
one of those devoted women whose thin,
worn face was beautiful because it told not
only of physical suffering but of spiritual
triumph.

Socialism amongst the women of the
Continent is more dogmatic, more aggressive,
than it is amongst ours, and that came out
at these Congresses. Storms blew—hurri-
canes sometimes struck the meetings in full
blast; but the revisionist British contin-
gent pursued its way steadily and persistently.
The movement in this country had to be
organised properly so that it might not be
misinterpreted abroad, and this was done
shortly before my wife's death, and mainly
by her own labours. Then the movement
abroad had to be interpreted to us. The

lot of the working women here is hard, but on the Continent in some respects it is harder. The grey veiling light of our moist atmosphere, which softens our landscapes and smooths out the hard outlines of division between object and object, seems to have a counterpart in our mental world, and that is not found abroad so much. Saint and sinner there stand in opposite well-defined camps with no neutral territory between, with no common meeting-ground where an evening can be spent under a truce, and where beneath the shadow of the olive-trees enemies may become friends. Here there are many such meeting places. Together we often discussed that. When my wife was reading this book for the first time, she told me that it explained so much to her, and that, had her lot been that which is here told, she would have considered it to be her mission to curse with a hardness and a bitterness of heart the society under which she was born. "We must have it in English," she said. "And if every rich and contented woman in the land would but read it, how wise she would become."

That will not happen. But it is a human document, written with that simplicity which is art triumphant. The tale needs no adornment of rhetoric and no pointing of

morals. It is a chapter torn from the book
of life, written as nature writes, and left
to produce its own effects on the mind of
whosoever will read. The critic of Socialist
doings and opinions whose life has been
as "a weel gaun mill," and whose mind
is like a stagnant backwater, has an easy
task when he sagely shakes his head over
the struggling eddies, the baffling currents,
and the splashy wavelets on the life of those
who are unhappy with fate, and who dream
of a fairer and juster world and imagine
that they can make their dreams come true;
but this book will explain many mysteries
to such a mind, and reveal many things
unmercifully hidden from it. "I remember
no tender words," Frau Popp says of her
youth, and one shivers as though looking
back over a desert which has just been
crossed. But romance, defying the barren-
ness of that youth, comes like a flower into
her life, and in her penury and distress she
begins to sigh over "unhappy queens." Then
she sighs over something more real and
more tragical—her fellow workers.

Adelheid Popp was born in 1869 at
Inzerschorf, near Vienna. At eight she
was earning money which was necessary for
family income. In 1891 she made the speech
to which she refers in this book, and three

years later she married. Two years before that she had been appointed Editor of one of the most influential women's papers published, the *Arbeiterinnen Zeitung* (Working Women's Newspaper), a Socialist organ. Amongst the many other positions she now holds is that of membership of the Managing Committee of the German Social Democracy in her native country. She has written much, and has been still more active on the platform. Altogether she is one of the most respected and influential of the Socialist women leaders on the Continent. Amongst Trade Unionists she is held in equal esteem, and the women's organisations are largely her creation. With all these cares and duties she manages the little family of two, which her husband left under her charge when he died in 1902, with a watchful affection which shows to those who know her privately how compatible public and domestic work are, and how she who seeks to mend the world is very often the woman who is most solicitous in guarding her own hearth.

J. RAMSAY MACDONALD.

INTRODUCTION TO THE GERMAN EDITION

WHEN the pastor without a pastorate, our present comrade, Goehre, in the beginning of the "nineties" brought out his work, "A Factory Worker for Three Months," in which he gives his experiences of the three months during which he played the part of a factory worker, one of the largest and most Conservative newspapers confessed that "we were better acquainted with the conditions of life of the half savage African tribes than with those of our own people."

This verdict might also be applied to the contents of the present work. It opens to the higher classes of the community a perfectly new world, but a world of such sorrow, misery, and such moral and spiritual deprivation, that we ask how such an existence is possible in our nation, so proud of its Christianity and civilisation.

The authoress portrays for us the lowest class on which our society is built—a class into which she was born and among which she lived for half a generation.

But we also see how in spite of her wretched environment she was able to set herself free, and working upwards to become a pioneer of her sex, esteemed and recognised as such to-day by all who know her.

I have seldom read a book with deeper emotion than this one of our comrade's. She pictures in burning colours the sufferings, the deprivations, and moral injuries of the life to which she as a poor child of the people was exposed, and which she, as a woman of the people, experienced doubly and to the bitter end.

She passes her childhood in a home which is not fit to be described as human; she possesses a father who is a drunkard and has no love for his family; she has a mother who is indeed good and diligent, who toils and drudges away all day long to keep her family above water, but who from anxiety for their daily maintenance, and in consequence of her poverty-stricken bringing up, is not only in-different, but inimical, to all spiritual interests, and cannot comprehend the struggles of her daughter to free herself from that lot unworthy of a human being into which fate has thrust her.

And she attained this freedom by her own strength, by strenuous diligence and untiring self-culture. She fills up the gaps in her scanty school education in an astonishing manner.

She bursts the bonds of the church in which she was fettered in her childhood, and becomes a free-thinker; the reverential believer in a monarchy becomes a republican; and the hard misery and experience of her life make her an enthusiastic Socialist and a champion for the emancipation of the whole proletariat.

Her life is thus an example for the imitation of many. She says, rightly, at the end of the narrative of her life that courage and self-confidence are necessary in order to make something of oneself. Many a fellow-worker could accomplish similar work if she were filled with zeal and enthusiasm for Socialism, striving to set mankind free.

I have one fault to find with the work—namely, that the authoress conceals her name from unjustifiable modesty. It will certainly not remain a secret, and I should consider it would be more effective for the circulation of the book if she, whose name everybody knows, would say openly: " So was I once, so am I now. I was impelled to do what I did; you others could do the same if you only wished."

May the circulation of this book run into its tens of thousands!

A. BEBEL.

SCHONEBERG, BERLIN,
22nd February 1910.

PREFACE TO THE THIRD EDITION

By the Author

I HAVE to thank August Bebel most heartily for undertaking the responsibility of publishing the story of my youth, and for guaranteeing the genuineness of the representation and the accuracy of the narrative. He dissuaded me from letting the book appear without my name. It was not exaggerated modesty, as he supposes, which stopped my coming forward with the story of my youth under my own name. I did not write the narrative because I esteemed it of some individual importance, but, on the contrary, because I recognised in my lot that of hundreds of thousands of the women and girls of the working class, because I saw great social phenomena at work in what surrounded me and brought me into difficult situations. I was not mistaken, as is proved by the numerous letters which I received from working women who see in my lot an image of their own.

When the second edition of this little book appeared, friends advised me no longer to withhold my name, as it had already become known, with no unfriendly intention, even if against my wish. But I refused, because I still hoped that the little book would have an effect as the autobiography of one working woman, which is at the same time that of hundreds of thousands. Now when the third edition is going forth I cannot help thinking that my purpose might not be understood, that readers will not understand why the little book does not bear my name, as the authorship is known to a far wider circle than I could have supposed. Now that my name stands in the book I need not keep silence on many a point which I did not introduce before because I feared that the authorship might thereby be discovered. I have been able to suppress in the third edition many passages which were to mislead friends and comrades from guessing at the author's name. Instead of these I have introduced new material. Fresh personages step into the circle of my narrative. I have mentioned my all too short married life, not in order to speak about myself, but to show by my individual experience that the public activity of a woman must not be hampered by her marriage and duties as wife and mother. This is connected with one of the greatest problems of the woman's question, one of the most important preliminaries in the discussion as to the qualifications of woman for perfect political and social equality with men.

ADELHEID POPP.

22nd February 1910.

THE AUTOBIOGRAPHY OF A WORKING WOMAN

MOST persons, if they have grown up under normal conditions, look back in times of heavy distress, with gratitude and emotion to their happy, beautiful, careless youth, and sigh, perhaps wishing: "If it could only come again!"

I face the recollections of my childhood with other feelings. I knew no point of brightness, no ray of sunshine, nothing of a comfortable home in which motherly love and care guided my childhood. In spite of this I had a good, self-sacrificing mother, who allowed herself no time for rest and quiet, always driven by necessity and her own desire to bring up her children honestly and to guard them from hunger. What I recollect of my childhood is so gloomy and hard, and so firmly rooted in my consciousness, that it will never leave me. I knew nothing of what delights other children and causes them to shout for joy—dolls, playthings, fairy stories, sweetmeats, and Christmas-trees, I only knew the great room in which we worked, slept, ate, and quarrelled. I remember no tender words, no kisses, but only the anguish which I endured as I crept into a corner or under the bed when a domestic scene took place, when my father brought home too little money and my mother reproached him. My father had a hasty temper; when roused he would beat my mother, who often had to flee half clad to take shelter with some neighbour. Then we were some days alone with the scolding father, whom we dared not approach. We did not get much to eat then; pitying neighbours would help us till our mother returned, impelled by anxiety for her children and household. Such scenes occurred nearly every month, and sometimes oftener. My whole heart clung to my mother; I had an unconquerable dread of my father, and I never remember to have spoken to him or to have been addressed by him. My mother told me later that he was vexed because I, the only girl of five to live, had dark eyes like hers.

I can still remember one Christmas Eve when I was not quite five years old. For this once I nearly obtained a Christmas-tree. My mother wanted just once to show me, her youngest child, what the Christ Child was. For many weeks she had constantly striven to save a few farthings in order to buy me some little cooking utensils. The Christmas-tree was adorned with chains of coloured paper, gilded nuts, and hung with modest playthings. We waited for our father to light the candles; he had gone to the factory to deliver some goods. He was to bring money home. Six o'clock struck, then seven, then eight—our father did not come. We were all hungry and wanted our supper. We were obliged to eat the nice poppy balls, apples, and nuts, to eat without our father, after which I went to bed without seeing the candles burn on the Christmas-tree. My mother was too much put out and anxious to light up the tree. I lay sleepless in my bed. I had looked forward so much to the Christ Child, and now he stayed away. At last I heard my father come; he was not received kindly, and another angry scene took place. He had brought less money than my mother expected, for he had visited a public-house on his way. He had nearly six miles to go, and he wanted to warm himself. He had then sat longer than he intended, and came home tipsy. At the noise which ensued I looked from my sleeping place—and then I saw how my father cut the Christmas-tree to pieces with a hatchet. I dared not scream; I only wept—wept till I fell asleep.

The next day my father felt some pity for me, for he gave me a few pence to buy tin kitchen things for myself. Compassionate persons gave me an old doll and playthings of their children's which had been discarded for other, more beautiful gifts.

And I can remember one other Christmas present. When I was a school-girl, a rich man, who possessed a great factory in which several hundred men and women worked, instituted a presentation of Christmas gifts for poor school children. I belonged to the fortunate ones who were presented with sweet-meats and articles of clothing. The great, giant fir-tree gave more light than I had ever seen, and the feast given us made us all happy. How grateful I was to the good, rich man who had such a compassionate heart for the poor. When my widowed mother later was obliged to work for twelve hours a-day in his factory at a weekly wage of six shillings, I could not believe that therein lay the source of his generosity.

I only attained this knowledge much later.

.   .   .   .   .   .

My father was struck with a malignant illness—cancer—which brought us into great poverty. He would not remain in the hospital;

but he was obliged to have medical help and medicines, and these swallowed up nearly all our earnings, and our circumstances became worse and worse. As often as I was sent to the chemist's with a prescription my mother complained as to how long it would last. One day he was so ill that the clergyman was fetched to confess him and to give him the last sacraments. That was a great event for me. All the inmates of the house knelt in our room and we with them. The smell of the incense filled the air, and the sobs of my mother were audible between the prayers. My father died a few hours later. My mother never forgot that he died without a word of reconciliation with her or of remembrance for his children.

I felt no sorrow when I wore the black clothes, the hat and veil lent me by a well-to-do family; I rather felt a sense of satisfaction at being so well dressed for once.

My mother was now the breadwinner for her five children. My eldest brother was indeed eighteen years old, but he could be no support to us, as he had learned a trade that was decaying. He resolved to try his fortune abroad, and went off. Two brothers, who till now had worked with their father, were apprenticed; the youngest, a child of ten, went to school.

My mother had great strength of will and much innate good sense. She was inspired with a wish to show that a mother can also provide for her children. Her task was most difficult, as she had learned nothing but domestic work. An orphan early, she had gone out to service at six years old; she had never been to school, and could, therefore, neither read nor write. She was also an enemy of the "new-fangled laws," as she called compulsory education. She considered it unjust for other men to dictate to parents what they were to do for their children. On this point my father had sympathised with her, and my brothers, when ten years old, had to help him in his work-weaving. Three years' schooling was sufficient, according to my parents' ideas; one of their frequent sayings was that he who had learned nothing when ten years old would learn nothing later. My youngest brother must now leave school; but meanwhile the law as to school attendance had become more firmly established, and the school authorities made difficulties. After many visits, my mother succeeded in getting permission for him to leave school and go into a factory as an assistant.

My brother was a diligent boy, and strove to earn as much as possible. He worked overtime till late in the evening, and in the summer went on Sundays to act as a skittle boy—to set up ninepins—for which he was also paid. He was thus all Sunday, often into the night, at public-houses, and was a witness of the wild orgies which usually form the end of such Sunday pleasures. In the hunting season he went with other boys as beaters for hare-hunting. Later he was apprenticed in our village, where he was very comfortable. One day he came home complaining—he had fallen on the ice and hurt his knee. That was for him the beginning of a very painful, lingering illness.

When the pain became increasingly severe he had to be taken to a hospital, from which he returned home in a few weeks. He went again to work; then a small lump came near his left ribs, which grew to the size of an egg, and one day broke whilst he was at work.

Now a bad time began for him and for all of us. There was the sick brother, and no wages coming into the house. My mother had no work, and the brother next to the youngest had run away from his master because he had been so cruelly treated. This was in a winter, too, in which no snow fell for a long time, so that nothing could be earned by sweeping away this bread from heaven. My mother shirked no trouble in order to find work. Sometimes she would wash clothes

somewhere, and then I had to go to her at
noon and she would share her meal with me.
We used to fetch from the restaurants the
water in which the sausages were cooked;
this with bread made an excellent tasty soup
for us. My sick brother received from compassionate neighbours soup and many other
good things. All tried to cure him. All good
and bad household remedies were tried. My
mother brought an ointment from the town,
which had been prepared by an old woman
and was to have wonderful results. Others
came and laid dry, pounded plums, mixed
with sugar, on his wounds. Herb baths were
made for him, so-called sympathetic treatments
were tried—all in vain; his wounds did not
heal. Then I was obliged to begin to help
earn. I knitted stockings for other people,
and ran messages. We worked at anything
that was offered us to avoid succumbing to
our need.

When the brother next to the youngest at
last found work with a mother-of-pearl worker,
I was bidden there to mind the children.
Finally I was taught how to sew on buttons,
and I now sewed mother-of-pearl buttons on
to silver and gold paper. That was always
my occupation when I was out of school or
during the holidays. When I had sewn on
144 buttons (a gross) I had earned one and a

half Kreuzer (nearly a farthing and a half). I never managed to earn more than twenty-seven Kreuzer in a week.

On New Year's Day I had to go round our village and the neigbourhood wishing people a Happy New Year. This was a custom practised by the poorest of our population. We only went to families known to be rich or comfortably off and expressed our good wishes for the New Year, for which we received a reward. I was terribly afraid of the dogs that guarded the houses of the rich; but I was also eager to bring home as much money as possible. I often went to a door from which another child was coming out on the same unsuitable errand. If a schoolfellow died in one of the better-off families, a number of poor children were chosen, who followed the coffin in a special procession. For that we received a payment of ten Kreuzer. Once when I could not go to school on account of my bad shoes the schoolmistress sent word that I ought nevertheless to go to the funeral of a rich schoolfellow, as I should receive for this mark of sympathy the small sum arranged. And I walked along the long, dirty, soaking road in shoes that had no soles to gain these few pence.

At this time, when we were in such great poverty, we heard a good deal of talk about a duchess who lived in a castle in a village about three miles off. People spoke much of her benevolence. She was said to have already made many men happy by her generosity. All that I had heard in fairy tales seemed embodied in this woman. My mother had a petition written, to be signed by the burgomaster and the pastor. It was not long before we received a gift of ten shillings. My mother was extremely happy at this help, and wondered how she could send her thanks for it.

The question was now debated as to whether I might not receive shoes if the Duchess knew how bad mine were. I was made to write a letter, which ran somewhat after this fashion :—

"Most Gracious Duchess,—As my mother does not know how to write, I am writing to tell you that she wishes to thank you most humbly for the five florins. I am ten years old, and often cannot go to school because I have no shoes. And I like going to school so much."

I expected a message from the Duchess from day to day, as from a fairy bringing a fortune. And it came. A message came that I should go to the headmistress of the village where the castle was. She sent me to a shoemaker, who took my measure for new shoes. A week later I was to fetch them from the castle. The schoolmistress taught me beforehand that I should say "Your Grace," or if I could not remember the words, "Most gracious Lady."

And so I tramped thither over the road, half covered with snow, that led to the castle. I wore wooden shoes on my feet, a green dress, and over my thin jacket I had fastened a shawl of my mother's. Excited, my heart beating anxiously, I approached the castle through the grove of magnificent, ancient trees. Even the walls which surrounded it inspired me with feelings which I should describe to-day, perhaps, as feelings of nervous awe. The porter, as the people called him, let me in, and sent me up a broad, magnificent staircase. Carpets were laid down such as I had never seen in any house, green plants adorned the walls. A gentleman received me at the top, who was magnificently dressed. He wore stockings to his knees and a coat trimmed with gold lace. That must be the Duke, I thought, and I hastened to kiss his hand as my mother had impressed on me to do. He turned away, and I learned later that he was the groom of the chambers. He led me on, and we passed a door through whose panels I saw a girl who looked just like me. She was dressed in a similar green frock, and had just such a shawl as mine. On her feet she had exactly the same wooden shoes as I wore. The girl had also eyes and hair as dark as mine.

I told my mother about it, and we racked our brains to think who it could be. As we had no notion of doors with mirrors let in them—for I had seen myself in one—we did not guess the riddle. The groom told me to wait in a corridor adorned with pictures. Soon a young lady appeared, who seemed to me as beautiful as an angel. She took me kindly by the hand, and led me into a great room whose walls were lined with books. For the first time I stood on a floor that was as slippery to walk upon as ice. The Duchess put me on a chair, and herself brought from an adjoining room the shoes destined for me, which I put on at her command. She pitied me on account of my thin jacket, and gave me a card, which I was to take to the schoolmistress, and which contained an order to have a warm jacket made for me. When I fetched the jacket the Duchess asked me about our circumstances, and I told her of my sick brother. She promised to send a doctor, and gave me money for my mother. As I gave a joyous assent to the question as to whether I enjoyed reading, she sent me books—one great book, beautifully bound, of which, strange to say, I have forgotten the title. A single sentence remains in my memory of the tale, "The Stolen Treasure." Then there was a book of Ottilie Wildermut's, with wonderfully beautiful pictures. Alas! I was obliged to sell the books when poverty and hunger again visited our home. I would willingly have bought them back later when I could judge of the educative value of books; but all my endeavours were vain. The Duchess kept her promise and sent her physician to my brother. The sad result of the examination was that he decided the home nursing was insufficient, and recommended the infirmary as the only place for saving him. And so it happened. My brother lay for more than a year on a water bed. Only so could he bear his ever increasing pain. His poor body looked fearful. He was very comfortable in the infirmary. They all treated him kindly, and he could not talk enough of all the many good things he had to eat. Everybody loved him. Other patients, when they left the hospital cured, used to come with presents for him. His nurses decorated his bed with flowers when he had been in it three hundred days. Everybody presented him with gifts. Yet he longed to come home again. He often begged us to write to the Duchess to take charge of him so that he might be with his mother. But we knew from the doctors that this was quite out of the question, and so we pacified him again. One day one of his nurses came to tell us that he was free from his terrible sufferings. He was buried in a pauper's coffin.

My mother had received work in the spring in the garden of the Duchess, by which our situation was somewhat improved. But now my many faulty attendances at school were punished. As my mother could not write, I had not often had a written excuse for my absence. The school authorities had had a return of the attendances, and my mother was condemned to twelve hours' imprisonment. As she had now work, she neglected to comply with the injunction to take her place for the "punishment." She also deemed it incredible that they would imprison her, an honest woman, who had always conducted herself honourably. But at six o'clock in the morning on Easter Saturday two policemen appeared and took her away. She was almost out of her mind at having such shame put upon her as being forced to walk through the streets between two policemen. She could only find comfort in the knowledge that her whole life was spotless and pure. Afterwards she was bidden to the headmaster, and he represented to her that she ought to send me regularly to school, as I was very gifted. She was also assured that "something might be made of me." My guardian was also made to come. But he contented himself with admonishing me to be good and pious. But of what use was it to go to school when I had neither clothes nor food?

When this year's schooling was over, my mother decided to migrate to the town. I was now ten years and five months old, and I was no longer to go to school, but to work. People dissuaded my mother from moving; they thought that if we remained in our village the Duchess might have me taught something. And really I had imagined it in my dreams. I had already pictured myself as a housemaid, as I was told the girl was called whom I often saw at the castle, prettily dressed with charming white aprons and ribbons. I would also have liked to be a schoolmistress, and I saw my ideal in my schoolmistress—a pretty, graceful girl, whose tasteful dress I had often admired. For a long time all sorts of fantastic ideas had pursued me, which all depended on the Duchess. As I had to work diligently all day, I was always thinking of her, and I dreamed that she would remember me, and appear to me, as in a fairy tale, bringing abundance of happiness and splendid things. These dreams remained dreams.

I do not know now why all intercourse with the castle ceased, why all the kindnesses we received came to an end. The one thing I still know is that we had many wants. Report made the few florins we received here and there into great riches. People prized the sympathy the Duchess showed us so highly that other poor women came to ask me to write petitions. The Duchess recognised my handwriting in the petitions of others, and asked me questions about the petitioners, who afterwards received substantial assistance. Then a report spread that the Duchess had been told we no longer needed help, as my mother had well-to-do sons. My mother went herself to the castle to contradict this report; but if suspicion is once aroused, it is very hard to allay it. My well-to-do brothers! Where and what were they? The one was a mechanic's assistant on the tramp; the second was serving a five years' apprenticeship in a distant village; a third was at home, and worked as a mother-of-pearl turner; and poor Albert was dying. It was said that the Duchess had often been taken in. Many stories were told of the experiences she had in visiting the homes of those who had begged for help in order to prove the genuineness of their stories. Thus, they said, she once went to a family who had described their need to her, and found them all feasting on roast goose. That is not always a sign of being well off, as I know from my own experience. I ate my first chicken when things were at a very low ebb with us. We had bought it at a great poulterer's shop, where they sold poor people the chickens that had died for a few pence. One New Year's Day my mother bought an old fowl for making soup for five-pence. Possibly something like this happened with the roast goose.

The Duchess had disappeared out of my life.

.   .   .   .   .   .

I received my removal certificate at school, which declared that I was ready to go into the fourth class of the elementary school. This was my sole equipment for the life of work which I was now to begin. No one protested against my being withdrawn from the legal eight years of school attendance. I was not registered on the police books. As my mother could not write, I was obliged to fill up the registration form. I ought, of course, to have entered myself under the heading "Children," but as I did not consider myself a child—I was a working woman—I left this heading not filled in, and remained unregistered by the police. Other people did not observe this omission.

We moved to the town, to an old married couple's, into a little room, in one corner of which was their bed, and in another my mother's and mine. I was taken into a workshop where I learned to crochet shawls. I earned from fivepence to sixpence a-day, working diligently for twelve hours. If I took home work to do at night, it was a few farthings more. I used to run to my work at six o'clock in the morning, when other children of my age were still sleeping. And they were going to bed, well fed and cared for, when I was hastening home at eight in the evening. Whilst I sat bent over my work, making one row of stitches after another, they played, or went for a walk or to school. I took my lot then as a matter of course; only one eager desire came to me again and again—just for once to have my sleep out. I wanted to sleep till I woke of my accord—that seemed to me to be a most splendid and beautiful thing. If I had sometimes the good fortune to be able to sleep on, it was indeed no happiness, for want of work or illness was the reason for it. How often on cold winter days, when my fingers were so stiff in the evening that I could no longer move my needle, I went to bed with the consciousness that I must wake up all the earlier. Then after my mother had wakened me she gave me a chair in the bed, so that I might keep my feet warm, and I crocheted on from where I had left off the previous evening. In later years a feeling of unmeasured bitterness has overwhelmed me, because I knew nothing, really nothing, of childish joys and youthful happiness.

The old couple with whom we lived were of very doubtful character. The woman lived by telling young girls and women their fortune by cards. She let me see into my future, which she painted in the most beautiful colours by means of the cards. This woman might have had great influence over me. She flattered me—a child ten years old—decked me with ribbons, and gave me sweet-meats. I might always have them all, she assured me, only my mother must know nothing about them. She urged me to do many things which I dared not venture to do because they seemed to me wrong. Fortunately my mother was suspicious, and we hired a tiny room which we had to ourselves. My younger brother also came to us, and brought a friend with whom he shared his bed. So we were four persons in a room which had not even a window, but which was lighted by panes of glass in the door. Once when a servant girl we knew was out of a situation, she came to us and slept with my mother, and I had to lie at their feet with mine on a chair pushed against the bed.

I crocheted shawls for a year, and learned to know a number of workshops; for when we heard that a farthing more a shawl was paid elsewhere, I was obliged to go there. I was thus always in fresh surroundings and among different persons, and could not get properly accustomed to any place. I also obtained an insight into many family histories. The proceeds of the sweating of so many young girls formed everywhere the foundation of the living of whole families. I frequently worked for the wives of officials or the employees of commercial businesses who could only keep up an appearance suitable to their station by the exploitation of our labour. I was always the youngest of all, and in order not to be worse paid on account of my youth, I gave myself out to be older, which I could do very well, as I was tall for my age, and my serious looks also made me appear older. Moreover I was obliged to be reckoned as older lest any one should guess that I ought actually to be at school.

I was in my twelfth year when my mother

decided to apprentice me. I was to learn a trade from which it was supposed a better wage could be obtained with diligence and dexterity—lacework. Of course, on account of my being of school age, I was again obliged to go to a middlewoman. For twelve hours a-day I was obliged to make ornaments out of pearls and silk lace for ladies' ready-made clothes. I received no fixed wage, but with every new article it was calculated exactly how many could be made in an hour, and I was paid five farthings for that number. When we had attained greater dexterity, and thereby were able to earn more, our employer reduced our wages on the ground that the manufacturer also paid less. We had to work continuously without being allowed a moment's rest. But this could not be expected from a child of my age, nor can it be done by any one, as every person knows who can himself judge what twelve hours of unremitting toil means. With what longing I looked at the clock when my pricked fingers pained me and when my whole body felt tired out! And when I went home on beautiful, warm summer days, or in the bitterly cold winter, I was often obliged, if there were much to do, to take home some work for the night. I suffered most from that, because it deprived me of the only pleasure I had.

I loved to read. I read without choice

whatever came into my hands, whatever acquaintances lent me—they did not distinguish between what was suitable and unsuitable for me—and whatever I could borrow at a second-hand bookshop in our suburb by paying a halfpenny, which I saved from my money for food. Stories of Indians, romances hawked about the streets, newspaper stories— I took them all home. In addition to stories of robbers, which particularly fascinated me, I was extremely interested in the stories of unhappy queens. Besides "Rinaldo Rinaldini" (which was my particular favourite), "Katerina Kornaro," "Rosa Sandor," "Isabella of Spain," "Eugénie of France," "Mary Stuart," and others, the "White Lady in the Imperial Palace" in Vienna, all the romances of the Emperor Joseph, "The Heroine of Worth," and "Emperor's Son and Barber's Daughter," gave me historical information. To them were added novels of the Jesuits and stories, in a hundred parts, of a poor girl who, after overcoming many and horrible difficulties, became a countess, or at least the wife of a manufacturer or merchant. I lived as if in a dream. I devoured number after number. I was withdrawn from real life, and identified myself with the heroines of my books. I repeated to myself all the words they spoke, and felt with them their terror when they were imprisoned, buried alive, poisoned, slain with a dagger, or smothered. I was continually with my thoughts in quite another world, and neither saw nor felt anything of the misery around me, nor felt my own. As my mother could not read, no one exercised any supervision over my reading. So I read Paul de Kock; but the frivolous French tales left me so harmless that I related the contents down to the smallest details, and did not understand why my brother and his friend laughed where I found nothing amusing. I have always remembered one passage. A marquis had led a girl into a wood, and then it went on: "When they came out again the girl was walking, pale and with faltering steps. She cast one last look back on the place where she had lost her innocence." The two young men laughed, without my finding a reason for it.

I narrated these stories very often. I could narrate very exactly, and knew many dialogues almost word for word, as if I had learnt them by heart. On Sunday evening I was invited to my employer's to read aloud to them. "The Love Adventures of Isabella of Spain," was the book read. In the house where we lived I was invited by the inmates to recite, and my mother and brother were really cruel to me from their desire to hear me recite. When all were in bed I was obliged to tell them stories; the others went to sleep, but I could not sleep, and I lay awake in bed in an excited state, in which I dared not move for fear of disturbing my mother. Besides, I would often rather have employed the time in reading if I was not obliged to work.

On Sunday afternoon, after I had helped in the morning in our modest household work, I read uninterruptedly till it was dark. In the summer I used to take my book to the cemetery, where I stayed, resting under a weeping willow, for hours, without paying attention to anything beyond my book. How I hated the Sunday work which I often had to do! Such a day I looked upon as lost, and the better supper and the little glass of wine or beer which I received as compensation did not seem such to me.

I was apprenticed for two years, and experienced in that time much mortification, harshness, and heartlessness. I was made use of as a kind of Cinderella. I was obliged on Saturday to do the cleaning work, and even to-day I feel the indignation I felt then when I remember how much was exacted from me and how I was treated. I was obliged to fetch the water in a heavy wooden jar from the public spring some distance off. We had no water laid on to the house then, and I did not dream that such a convenience could exist. Strange men often pitied me, and helped me to

carry my jar. My mistress went on the prin-
ciple, "I must accustom you to everything,"
"for you will never be a great lady," said she.

The two children played me all the mis-
chievous tricks of which they were capable.
They joked at my poverty, and made merry
because I had to go barefoot in summer,
which mortified me bitterly. But, as it was
only a few steps to go, my mother considered
wearing shoes on week days extravagant for
such a child. As the trade which I was learning
was dependent on the season, there were some
weeks twice in the year when little, and for a
time even no work was to be done. Then I
read through all the shop announcements, and
where I could guess girls might be wanted
I went in. That was the hardest thing of
all. Always the same stereotyped question:
"Please, I would like some work." I can feel
to-day in all its intensity the humiliating feeling
which I experienced in my anxious and yet
expectant plea for work. I was often obliged
to dry the hot, flowing tears before I was able
to speak.

Once, when I was over thirteen and looked
almost grown up, I came in my search for work
to the office of a manufacturer of bronze goods.
A little, old man, who was the chief himself,
asked my name, age, and family history, and
engaged me for the following Monday. I

received a place among twelve young girls, and was once more in a warm, heated room. I was shown how to string chain links, and soon acquired some dexterity. The chief was kind to me. I was here also the youngest workwoman, but I soon earned more than I had received as an apprentice. The apprentice work was now quite given up, as the new work seemed more profitable. I worked ten months uninterruptedly in the bronze factory. I received, according to my ideas at that time, nice clothes, ventured to buy pretty shoes, and also many things which please young girls.

My chief was very kind to me, and made a favourite of me. He spoke in a truly fatherly manner, and confirmed me in my resolve to keep away from all the pleasures which attracted my fellow-workers. The girls went to dances on Sundays, and gave accounts of them. In the intervals they amused themselves with the young workmen; although I did not understand the meaning of their talk, I had the feeling that one ought not to talk so. I was often laughed at because I was so much alone; but, as I was always ready to recite in the intervals between work, they were not unkind to me in any other way.

After some months another kind of work was assigned to me which was better paid, but it was harder. I had to solder with a pair of bellows driven by gas, which did not appear to do me any good. My cheeks grew paler and paler, a great unconquerable feeling of tiredness overcame me, and I had giddy attacks, and often had to sit down.

Another event much upset me at that time. I have already mentioned that we did not live alone, but that a comrade of my brother's lived with us. He—an ugly man of few words, marked by small-pox—began to pay me attentions. He would bring me harmless presents such as fruit and pastry. He also procured books for me. Neither my mother nor I thought anything of it—I was only just fourteen years old. Once, on a holiday, he came home in the evening, and we went to bed before my brother came. I lay beside my mother, next the wall. I was not quite fast asleep when I suddenly woke with a cry of terror. I had felt a hot breath above me, but in the darkness could not see what it was. My scream had wakened my mother, who immediately struck a light and perceived what it was. The man had raised himself in his bed, the foot of which was against the head of ours, and had bent over me. I trembled with fright and anguish, and without rightly knowing what he was thinking of, I felt instinctively that it was something wrong. My mother reproached him, and he scarcely replied. When my brother came home, whom we stayed awake to receive, there was a terrible scene, and his comrade was given notice to quit. What I had expected and desired did not happen. He was not sent away immediately, but allowed to remain till the end of the week in order to have time to look for another sleeping place and not to be sent away in disgrace. I was afraid to fall asleep, and when I did I had the most horrid dreams. I flung my arms round my mother to feel safe. I was scolded for being over excited; the novels which I had read were considered the cause of it, and I was forbidden to read any more.

Some weeks after this alarming occurrence I was seized with a very severe fainting attack. When I had recovered consciousness, with the doctor's help, terrible ideas tormented me. The doctor considered the case very serious, and pronounced it to be a nervous illness, and at the hospital to which my mother took me questions were asked as to the manner of life of my father and grandfather, and the doctors considered my father's immoderate enjoyment of alcohol the cause of my illness. They found me under nourished and bloodless to the last degree, and advised much exercise in the open air and good nourishment. How was I to follow their orders?

.   .   .   .

All that I had hitherto suffered from deprivation, work, and mortification was surpassed in the following months. I was not allowed to return to the bronze factory, as the physicians said it would be poison to me. After my health had apparently improved, I had again to look for work. But I lived in constant fear. I was afraid to go a step alone from the house, for I had constantly the feeling of losing consciousness. To be able to die was my dearest wish. But I must look for work. When I found work, and had entered my situation, anxiety overwhelmed me. I used to spend the dinner interval in the park, as I ought to have as much fresh air as possible. I took my dinner there—fruit and bread or a piece of sausage—the "good nourishment" which the physicians had recommended for me. It was now more scanty than before, because I had earned nothing for some weeks, and the doctor, who had been fetched at the first alarm, and the chemist had both to be paid. No insurance against sickness had then been started.

I had not been allowed to remain in the bronze factory because the work was undermining my health; but now I was working in a metal factory, where I had to tend a press, and where I, as the latest comer, had to carry up the burning material from the underground room, always tormented by the fear of fainting in climbing or descending the bad stairs. I was only a few days there, and then found work in a cartridge factory. When I had been there three weeks, and was going along the streets at noon, I had to be supported by passers-by, as I began to totter, and I again became unconscious. When the faint was over they took me home, and frightened my mother. I begged her to get me into the hospital, which might cure me, if anything could do so.

As they were not clear what was the matter with me, I was taken to the mental hospital. Half a child still, I was not aware of the fearful significance of being obliged to live with the mentally afflicted. It was, paradoxical as it may sound, the best time I had ever had. Every one was kind to me—the doctors, the nurses, and also the patients. I received good food several times a-day — often even roast meat and jam, which I had never tasted till then. I had a bed to myself, and always clean linen. I made myself useful to the nurses — helped them in cleaning the rooms and in serving the invalids in bed. I sewed and knitted for them. Then I read books which one of the doctors lent me. At that time I became acquainted with the works of Schiller and Alphonse Daudet. The dramatic works of Schiller, and especially the "Bride of Messina," pleased me most. Daudet's "Fromont Junior and Risler Senior" made the greatest impression on me. My trouble, which had made me so unhappy, did not show itself whilst I was in the hospital. I grew strong and looked blooming. I constantly prayed quietly to be freed from my anxiety, and I used to fall asleep praying. In my room were only quiet patients suffering from depression and melancholia. Two young girls were there who informed me they had been brought to the hospital. In one case a cruel father was said to have separated his daughter from her lover, in the other a guardian had been guilty of diabolical acts against his ward. I believed all that was told me, and mourned with those who were sad. In the garden we came across other patients, who were really mad. One woman imagined herself to be Elizabeth of Mexico. She always stood on one spot and spoke in a loud voice, as a queen to her subjects. Another thought she had committed murder, and was afraid of being prosecuted. In these surroundings I remained four weeks, and was then discharged as cured.

The search for work began again. I left home early in the morning to be the first at the gates, but it was always a vain quest.

My mother had been exceedingly kind to me from the time of my illness, and often called me her poor, unhappy child. She received with emotion the caresses she had formerly repelled. She had repelled them not from want of love, but because she was convinced that flattery is another word for deceit. But now she became cross again because I was so long earning nothing. She had so much to do. She worked every day and all day long without any pause or rest. She worked in a weaving-mill. She had developed wounds in her fingers from the poisonous colours of the wool, and painful ulcers gathered in her arm; but she conquered every pain, and carried through her laborious, badly-paid day's work. And she was no longer a young woman. I, her fifteenth child, was born when she was forty-seven, so that she was now sixty-one, and during her whole life she had had no day of rest. If she had no work, she hawked soap or fruit in order to earn food for us. It was her ambition not to owe any rent or to be in debt for anything else. It was a special characteristic of hers to wish not to be dependent on any one. And now she had a great girl, who ought to be a support to her, and this girl was earning nothing. She reproached me bitterly, and scolded me; because she herself had always managed to earn money, I ought also to be able to do so.

I sought for all kinds of work. I tried for it in a cardboard box factory, in a shoe factory, at a fringe-maker's, in a workshop where fresh colours were worked on Turkish shawls, and in many other trades. After some hours they either found me not clever enough for the work, or I heard of some other work that was better paid and went after that.

Three weeks had passed in this way when the giddy attacks began again, and these were followed by a severe fainting fit. I went again to the hospital. I was so weak and exhausted that I roused general pity as we walked through the streets. We had often to stop at a house so that I might recover myself on the steps. I was feverish when I entered the hospital, and was sick after my first meal; but in a few days all was well again. I had again had good food and comforts such as I had not known elsewhere.

Then something happened, the whole horror of which I only learned to know in later years. One day I was told that there was no prospect of my becoming healthy and capable of continuous work, and, therefore, I must go into another institution.

I had to dress, get into the hospital ambulance, and in a few minutes I found

myself in the receiving room of the work-
house. I was exactly fourteen years and four
months old. I was not conscious of the meaning of the change; I only wept, wept un-
ceasingly at my surroundings. In a great
dormitory where rows of beds were arranged
side by side, mostly for old and decrepit
women, a bed and a cupboard were pointed
out for me. The old women coughed and
had attacks of choking; many were delirious,
and talked in the most extraordinary fashion.
At night I could not sleep because I was
again terribly frightened, the old women also
were restless, and did not always stay in their
beds. The food was not nearly so good as
in the hospital. Then I had nothing to do,
no needlework, no books—no one troubled
about me. I sought out the most lonely
paths in the great garden to be able to weep.
On the fifth day I was sent for to the Board
Room, where I was questioned as to whether
I had any one who could look after me, because
I could not stay there; and if no one would
look after me, I must return to my native
parish.

I did not know my native parish. I had
never lived there, and did not understand
the language spoken in it. I was quite
desperate, and the desire just to be able to
die again overwhelmed me. I stammered

that I had a mother who worked, and that I myself had worked since I was ten years old. I received a card on which I had to write that my mother must fetch me immediately, otherwise I should be sent to Bohemia. The next day I went home with my poor mother, who was never spared any hardship.

In later years I have often asked myself what would indeed have happened to me had I been sent to Bohemia, my native place. I began also to consider the criminality of bureaucratic routine, which placed me, a child, deprived through labour and hunger of all childish pleasures, in a home for old and infirm women, and which—but for the presence of a thoughtful official—would have delivered me over to a fearful lot, certainly for many years. A wave of bitterness came over me as I realised all this, and said to myself that it could only be ascribed to a mere accident that I, now a healthy working girl, and later a healthy woman, had not been thrust amongst people who would have treated me, at the best, as a troublesome stranger.

If the official had not seen me in my walks in the garden and spoken to me because he was struck with my youth, I should probably not have been spared heavy suffering. Now I was at home again, and had to learn white sewing.

. . . .

A month's tuition was arranged, and my mother willingly paid the fee asked for it, supported by the hope of procuring me better work. I came again to a middlewoman who employed a number of girls. The husband did not work; he spent most of his time in the coffee-house, and let his wife earn their living. The wife sweated the girls incredibly. I was to learn white sewing in four weeks; but what did I do instead? My mother had made for her circumstances enormous sacrifices to have me equipped for a better trade. She had arranged to dress me properly, had paid the teaching fee in advance, and fed me for four weeks. And I? I was turned into a children's nurse. I had no longer any feeling in my arm because I had to carry the middle-woman's small child so much. I had to go for walks for hours, so that the others should not be troubled by the children's screaming. I had to go shopping, wash crockery, and do all sorts of things that had nothing to do with the trade I ought to be learning. Only at the beginning of the fourth week did I begin to sew buttonholes, turn down hems, draw threads, and at last I was allowed to sit at the machine in order to attempt my first sewing *on paper*. I broke down in working the machine with my feet, and that was the art with which I should now earn my living and repay my mother for all she had done for me.

But my good teacher had no intention of allowing me to work with her in order, at least, to be taught what she had not taught me at first. Quite on the contrary; she was wanting another girl, to be able to make use of her for her child, and to be paid for doing so. She sent me away with the excuse that she had no work and could not employ me. My mother would not be satisfied with that; she demanded a return of her money or a repetition of the period of teaching. But every hour she wasted on these interviews meant loss of work and with it loss of money. So I had again to look about—this time for employment in white sewing. I could certainly have found work, but people saw by the first piece I took into my hands that I could do nothing, and there was an end of it. I was obliged again to take any work I could get.

But in order to obtain continuous work my mother spoke to my first mistress, who took me on again. But it was a particularly unfortunate year, as the fashions were developing in another direction. The dead season, which in other years begins only just before Christmas, began this year as early as November. At first we worked a few hours a-day, less but all work came to a standstill four weeks before Christmas. I was again at home, and I was a great girl of fifteen. Day after day I began again my wanderings We were particularly hard hit this time, as we had another member of our family without work. Whilst my younger brother had been called away to fulfil his time of military service, the elder brother had come back from the barracks. He was almost without the most necessary clothes, and without a penny of money, but he had a large appetite. And it was so difficult to find work, though he was ready to take up any kind. He would get something temporary, but he could find nothing permanent. And he was to be a help to us! We had so rejoiced at his coming home. There he was—a strong, healthy man after he had served his emperor and fatherland for three years—and he had to be kept by his old mother and a sister who was still half a child, and he had only scraps of food to eat. I certainly did not think of this at the time; I was only proud that my brothers were able to serve their emperor and to help defend their fatherland in case of war.

In this dark time all the advice given my mother was taken. I had to write petitions to the emperor, to archdukes, and to other rich "benefactors." I had to compose the petitions because, as I have already mentioned, my mother could neither read nor write, and I did it in my own fashion. I related the case quite simply. I began after the usual form of address, as once before to the Duchess: "As my mother cannot write, and we are so badly off." We received five florins from the emperor and the same amount from an archduke and a rich benefactor whose secretary came to enquire about us. Most of it went in buying the most necessary articles of clothing for my brother. But what to live on? My mother now earned four florins a-week, which had to keep three persons.

At any cost I must find work. The events which followed I shall never forget, and no year has passed since in which I have not remembered that particular Christmas.

.   .   .   .

It was a cold, severe winter, and the wind and snow could come into our room unhindered. When we opened the door in the morning, we had first to cut away the ice which had frozen to it in order to get out, for the entrance to the room was direct from the court, and we had only a single glass door. My mother left the house at half-past five, because she had to begin work at six. I went an hour later to look for work. "Please, I want work," must again be said innumerable times. I was in the streets nearly the whole day. We could not heat our room—that would have been extravagant—so I walked up and down the streets, into the churches, and to the cemetery. I took with me a piece of bread and a halfpenny with which to buy my dinner. It was always a great effort to keep back from weeping when my prayer for work was refused, and I had to go out again from the warm room. How willingly would I have done any work to stop my freezing so. My clothes became damp in the snow, and my limbs grew stiff after walking for hours. My mother became more and more angry about it. My brother had found work; snow had fallen, so he was busy, but for such a little pay that he could scarcely keep himself. I only had no work.

I even got no work in the sweetmeat factories, of which I had heard that they could make use of many hands at Christmas time. To-day I know that nearly all the Christmas work is done some weeks before the festive days, that for weeks before women must work day and night, and that they are dismissed before Christmas without any consideration. I had then no idea of how the process of production is arranged. With what piety and faith I prayed in church for work. I sought out the specially celebrated saints. I went from altar to altar, knelt down on the cold stone steps and prayed to the Virgin Mary, the Mother of God, the Queen of Heaven, and to other saints who were considered specially powerful and benevolent.

I did not give up hope, and I resolved one day to throw the couple of farthings I had for my dinner into the box for offerings to the Holy Father. On the same day I found a purse with twelve florins. I could scarcely contain myself for joy, and I thanked all the saints for this favour. It never occurred to me that some other poor creature might have been thrown into trouble by the loss of the purse. Twelve florins was to me such a large amount that I never even thought a poor man could have lost them. I knew nothing of the duty of taking things found to the police. I only saw the gracious, kindly hand of my saints in the purse lying on the path! On this evening I fell on my mother's neck rejoicing. I could not speak for joy, and could only bring out these words: "Twelve florins, I have brought you twelve florins."

Now proud joy had entered our room, and as if to make our good fortune complete, I was sent for the next day to enter a glass paper factory, in which I had a few days previously asked for work, and where they had made a note of my address.

My new work place was in the third storey of a house which was only used for business purposes. Up till now I had not been acquainted with the life and drive of a factory; and I had never felt so uncomfortable. Everything displeased me. The dirty, sticky work, the unpleasant glass dust, the many employees, the common tone, and the whole manner in which the girls and married women talked and behaved.

The manufacturer's wife, the "gracious lady," as she was called, was the actual manager of the factory, and she talked quite as much as the girls. She was a beautiful woman, but she drank brandy, took snuff, and made unseemly, rude jokes with the workmen. When the manufacturer, who was often ill, came himself, there was always a violent scene.

I pitied him. He seemed to me to be so good and noble that I concluded from his wife's behaviour that he must be unhappy. By his orders I was given another, much pleasanter, kind of work. Hitherto I had been obliged to hang the paper, smeared with glue and sprinkled over with glass, on the ropes which were stretched fairly high across the room. This work tired me very much, and the manufacturer must probably have noticed that it was not suitable for me, for he ordered that from now I should count over the paper that was to be worked upon. This work was clean, and pleased me much better. Certainly when there was nothing to count I had again to return to the other work. The factory was a good distance from our house, and I was not able to go home to dinner. Then I remained with the other employees in the work-room. We fetched soup or vegetables from the restaurant; for our dinner we had coffee as well. I always sat on one side and read in a book. I was reading " The Brigand and his Child," which was in a hundred parts. The others laughed at me, and joked at my innocence because their talk confused me.

They often talked of Mr Berger, the traveller for the firm, who was expected back now. All the women idolised him, so that I was very curious to see the man. I had been there a fortnight when he arrived. All was commotion, and the only talk was of the looks of the traveller. He came with the gracious lady into the room where I was working. In the afternoon I was called to the office. Mr Berger sent me for something, and made a stupid remark at the same time about my " beautiful hands." When I came back it was dark, and I had to pass an empty anteroom, which was not lighted, and was, therefore, half dark, as it only received light through the glass door leading into the work-room. Mr Berger was in the room as I came through. He took me by the hand and enquired sympathetically into my circumstances. I answered him truthfully, and told him of our poverty. He spoke very kindly, praised me, and promised to use his influence for me to get my wages raised. Naturally I was much pleased at the prospect held out to me, as I had only two and a half florins a-week, for which I worked twelve hours daily. I stammered a few words of gratitude, and assured him I would show myself worthy of his recommendation. Before I rightly knew what had happened, Mr Berger had kissed me. He sought to soothe my horror with the words : " It is only a fatherly kiss." He was twenty - six and I nearly fifteen, so that there could not be much question of fatherliness.

I hastened to my work quite beside myself. I did not know what to think of what had happened; I considered the kiss as something disgraceful, but Mr Berger had spoken so compassionately, and given me a prospect of higher wages. At home I spoke, indeed, of the promise, but I was silent about the kiss, as I was ashamed to talk of it before my brother. But both mother and brother rejoiced because I had found such an influential protector.

On the next day a fellow-worker—a young fair-haired girl, whom I had liked best of all of them—overwhelmed me with reproaches. She complained that I had taken her place with the traveller, that hitherto if anything had to be done or fetched for him she had done it. She assured me with sighs and tears that he had loved her, and that now all was at an end owing to me. The other girls joined in; they called me a hypocrite, and the gracious lady herself asked me how I liked the kisses of the "handsome traveller." They had seen what had taken place the previous evening through the glass door, and showed it in this (to me) humiliating manner.

I was defenceless against these gibes and scoffing speeches, and I longed for the hour when I could go home. It was Saturday, and when I received my wages I went home with the intention of not returning on Monday.

When I spoke of it at home I was severely scolded; it was curious. My mother, who had always been so much concerned to bring me up a well-conducted girl, who had always given me warnings and instructions not to talk to men—"only by one's future husband should one be kissed," had she impressed upon me,—she was in this instance against me. I was called over excited. A kiss was nothing bad, and if I received higher wages from it, it would be stupid to give up my work. Finally my books were again made answerable for my "over - excitement," and my mother was so angry at "my obstinacy" that the splendid books lent me—"The Book for All," "Over Land and Sea," "Chronicles of the Times,"—for "so far" had I advanced in literature—were thrown out of doors. I collected them all again, indeed; but I dared no longer read in the evenings, although on Saturday I had been allowed to read longer.

That was a sad Sunday. I was utterly cast down, and in addition I was scolded the whole day.

On Monday my mother woke me as usual, and impressed on me, as she went to work, not to be stupid, but to think that in a few days it would be Christmas.

I went out—I wanted to conquer myself and go into the factory; I came to the door, then I turned back. I had such a nameless dread of unknown dangers that I would rather starve than suffer disgrace. For all that had happened — the kiss and my comrades' reproaches—seemed to me disgrace. I had been told, moreover, that one of the girls was always in the traveller's special favour; and indeed he was changeable, for if a new girl came who pleased him better than the last, then she stepped into her place. According to all signs I had been chosen to step into the place. I had read in books so much about seduction and fallen virtue that I had created the most horrible fancies for myself. So I did not go in.

But what was I to do? At first I sought work—I would have taken anything that offered; but three days before Chrismas no fresh hands are wanted. I wandered about the streets, and when evening came I went home at the usual hour. I had not the courage to confess that I had not been to the factory. I did the same the two following days. All endeavours to find work were fruitless. Utter desperation took possession of me; then I hoped again that perhaps some accident might happen to help me. It was only a question of two florins, as it was not a whole working week.

I had read so much of the power of God, of help in the hour of need, of virtue rewarded, and similar things, that I persuaded myself that help would be given to me. Therefore I knelt before the altar in prayer, and then went to look for work. I might, indeed, find another purse and take home more money than was expected. I went where the women stood crowded together by the fish stalls to buy for their evening meal. Although I had always thought of fish as something very delicious, now in my desperation I had no longing for it. I only wanted money. Mad thoughts from the carrying out of which, however, I drew back with horror, passed through my head. Afternoon came. People were hurrying home with their parcels to prepare happy time for their dear ones. Signs festivity were everywhere. But where shall I get money?

A thought occurred to me. I had an aunt who was in service with a countess; this aunt was to us the personification of high rank, her situation with the Countess procured this halo for her. The "town aunt,"—that always sounded to us very splendid,—and when she occasionally visited us, we always paid her the highest deference. She was considered very pious, and the church, belonging to a certain Order, which she always attended, received many gifts from her. I now hoped for help from her. I did not find her at home; she was at church. I sought her there; she had already left. I knelt again at the altar, and prayed with tears and sobs that God and the saints would make the heart of my aunt incline towards me. When I now consider—I wanted scarcely two florins, and all my grief and heart trouble would have been over! I did not know at that time how much money is uselessly squandered, how many men live in luxury whilst others pine and want. At that time I did not know of this difference or I had not considered its injustice.

I have never forgotten these hours and all the suffering of my childhood and youth. And still, in spite of the many years which have passed since then, I can never pass weeping children without asking the cause of their tears. I always think in such cases of my own tears, and of how I needed pity. As a badly-paid working-woman I have often given the earnings of many hours' work to strange, weeping children who have told me of their need in the streets.

I found no pity. My pious aunt, whom I found at last, treated me hospitably to coffee and cakes, but when I finally ventured to present my petition, she remained hard and pitiless. She told me to go home directly, as it was Christmas Eve, and I should be expected. I begged and cried; it did not move her. In pious sentences she refused to help. Her last words were: " Every one must bear the consequence of his own deeds." So I again stood in the streets. Very few people were now to be seen, but the windows shone brilliantly, and I could see many decorated Christmas-trees.

I did not want to go home at all. What

should I say? I was afraid and ashamed. My behaviour the last few days seemed to be now very wrong. I imagined the horror of my mother—my poor, worried mother, who had to count every farthing, and who put so much hope in me. Could I cause her so much pain and disillusion? My remorse and anguish increased every moment. I said to myself: "Oh, that I had overcome my fears and stayed on in the factory!" My fear of the traveller, my shame at the girls' talk, and my anxiety about propriety—all seemed to be gross exaggeration. I felt now how delightful it would be if I were going home with the wages for my work. I turned into the road to the Danube, and I had a presentiment that it would be easier to jump into the water than to go home with my guilt.

As I was hastening through the better streets to my new goal—the water—whilst my tears flowed uninterruptedly and my sobs shook my whole body, I was addressed by a fine gentleman. He asked me whither I was going so late, and why I was crying. It must be my salvation, I thought; it must be a dispensation of Providence. Every hope revived in me, and I narrated my trouble. I must have two florins, otherwise I dared not go home. How kindly and nobly the gentleman spoke. He would give me ten florins, only I must go with him, as he had no money with him. I do not know what possessed me, but in spite of my need, I did not go to his house. When we came to the house, into which he wished to lead me, I begged to be allowed to remain outside till he came with the money. When he tried to persuade me and to draw me into the house, I broke loose and ran away. Such an inexpressible fear overcame me, the looks which the gentleman gave me had frightened me so much, that without considering what I was doing, I rushed away in the direction of my home.

There I met my brother, who had been looking for me a long time, and who was on the point of going to the factory to enquire for me.

Shall I now relate how the rest of this Christmas Eve passed? How neither mother nor brother could understand my feeling or emotions nor pardon me? They called me naughty and lazy. Lazy! At an age when other children play with dolls or go to school, when they are guarded and cherished so that they may not stumble over any obstacle—at this age I had to go out to bear the hard yoke of work. At an age when others are enjoying all the blessedness of childhood, I had already forgotten childish laughter, and was thoroughly imbued with the feeling that work was my destined lot.

The burden of this childhood influenced my disposition for a long time, and made me a creature disliking mirth from my earliest years. Much had to happen, something great had to step into my life to help me to conquer.

. . . .

I found work again; I took everything that was offered me in order to show my willingness to work, and I passed through much. But at last things became better. I was recommended to a great factory which stood in the best repute. Three hundred girls and about fifty men were employed. I was put in a big room where sixty women and girls were at work. Against the windows stood twelve tables, and at each sat four girls. We had to sort the goods which had been manufactured, others had to count them, and a third set had to brand on them the mark of the firm. We worked from 7 A.M. to 7 P.M. We had an hour's rest at noon, half-an-hour in the afternoon. Although there was a holiday in the week in which I began to work, I received the full wages paid to beginners. That was four florins. I had never yet been paid so much. Besides that, the prospect was held out to me after a few month's steady application of receiving an increase of a shilling. I received it in six weeks' time, and in six months I was earning ten shillings; later I received twelve shillings.

I seemed to myself to be almost rich. I reckoned how much I could save in the course of a year, and built castles in the air. As I had been accustomed to extraordinary privations, I should have considered it extravagant to spend more now on my food. If I only did not feel hungry, I never even considered of what my food consisted. I only wanted to be well dressed, so that if I went to church on Sunday no one should guess I was a factory worker. For I was ashamed of my work. Working in a factory had always seemed to me to be degrading. When I was an apprentice I had always heard it said that factory girls were bad, disorderly, and depraved. They were always talked about in the most scornful manner, and I had also adopted this false notion. Now I myself was going to a factory where there were so many girls.

The girls were kind; they instructed me in my work in the friendliest manner, and introduced me to the customs of the factory. The girls of the sorting room were considered the *élite* of the employees. The manufacturer himself selected them, whilst the engaging of those for the machine-room was left to the overseers. In the other rooms there were boys and girls together; but in my room there were only girls. Men only came in to assist us when the heavy parcels of sorted, counted, and marked goods had to be taken to the courtyard. We could take our dinner at noon in the factory. In fine weather we sat or reclined on the parcels of goods in the glass-covered courtyard, in the winter time we were allowed to go into the machine-room. We were not allowed to remain in the sorting-room, where it would have been much more comfortable to stay, because the goods would have absorbed the smell of our " food."

The girls living near the factory went home to dinner; and they had the best of it, because they could get a better and a warm dinner. For some weeks I dined with acquaintances. This was real torture. I had to walk quickly for twenty-five minutes, then swallow a hot dinner as fast as possible, and hurry back to work, arriving breathless and heated. I could not stand this for long, and I again stayed at the factory.

From the women of this factory one can judge how sad and full of deprivation is the lot of a factory worker. Here were the best recognised conditions of work. In none of the neighbouring factories were the wages so high; we were envied everywhere. Parents considered themselves fortunate if they could get their daughters of fourteen in there on leaving school. Every one strove to give perfect satisfaction to avoid being dismissed. Yes; the married factory girls struggled to introduce their husbands (who had learned a trade for years) into the factory as assistants, because their position was then safe. And even here, in this paradise, all were badly nourished. Those who stayed at the factory for the dinner hour would buy themselves for a few farthings a sausage or the leavings of a cheese shop. Many a time they ate bread-and-butter and cheap fruit. Some drank a glass of beer, and sopped bread in it. If we felt a loathing for the food, we fetched a meal from the restaurant. For $1\frac{1}{4}$d., either soup or vegetables. It was seldom well prepared and the smell of the fat was horrible. We often felt such a disgust for it that we threw it away, and preferred to eat dry bread, and comfort ourselves by thinking of the coffee which we had brought for the afternoon.

The employer often passed through the courtyard when we were taking our dinner. Many a time he stopped to ask what good things we had. If he were in a particularly good humour, or if the girl whom he addressed were pretty, and understood how to complain, he would give her money that she might buy something better. That always made me angry; it seemed to me humiliating, and provoked me.

We also tried going to an inferior kind of cookshop. There we received for twopence soup and vegetables. For a further twopence two girls would buy a piece of cooked meat between them. I went to a cookshop for some time when I was ill and the doctor said that good food was most necessary for me. But after my health had improved and I was stronger, I did not like the great expense. I wanted to save money, to have some ready when in need of it.

Moreover, only those girls could be better nourished who were helped by their families. But there were very few of these. Much oftener the girls had to support their parents or pay for the board of their children. How self - sacrificing these mothers were! They saved up one farthing after another to improve their children's lot, or to make presents to the foster mothers so that they might take good care of the children. Many women often had to earn for their husbands, who were out of work, and to undergo a double deprivation because they had to struggle alone to earn the money for their household expenses.

I also learnt to know the much-slandered levity of factory girls. Certainly some girls went to dances, some had love affairs; others took their places at three o'clock in the afternoon at a theatre, in order to be present at an evening performance, for 7½d. They took excursions in the summer, and walked an hour in order to save a halfpenny fare. They had, in consequence, to pay for the breath of country air by having tired feet for the whole day. All that may be called frivolity, even a thirst for pleasure or dissipation; but who has the courage to call it so?

I saw amongst my colleagues, the despised factory workers, instances of extraordinary self-sacrifice. If any special poverty was found in a family, they put their farthings together to help. When they had worked twelve hours in a factory, and when many had walked for an hour to get home, they would mend their clothes, though they had not been taught how to do so. They unpicked their dresses to make new ones from the old pieces, at which they sewed at night and on Sundays.

Even the intervals for meals were not devoted to rest. The eating of the scanty meal was quickly accomplished, and then stockings were knitted, crocheted, or embroidered. And in spite of all the dilligence and economy, every one was poor, and trembled at the thought of losing her work. All humbled themselves, and suffered the worst injustice from the foremen, not to risk losing this good work, not to be without food.

The misfortune happened to many a girl of

being the special favourite of one of the fore-men. Suddenly his behaviour would alter. She could no longer do anything right, she made no further progress; instead of an increase in wages she received only repri-mands. She was threatened with a notice to leave, and the poor girl was harassed until she could bear it no longer and left of her own accord.

Reports were circulated about some to whom this had happened. One whispered to another that they had been seen in certain streets gaudily dressed, or they had been seen leaning out of windows enticing men. They were always blamed, and I was also filled with indignation. No one thought if it would have been different if the girl had given up resistance quite at the beginning and yielded to the foreman.

I knew then nothing of secret or public prostitution. I had never yet heard the word. Later, when I could better judge of cause and effect, I learnt to think differently of these girls, especially when, in the course of the years during which I worked in the factory, I learnt to know many working women of whom it was told to what relations with the foremen they owed their favoured position. Or when others made scenes with a foreman, because he began suddenly to oppress them, as he was tired of them, and wanted them out of his way in order to be able, unhindered, to favour another woman.

At that time I did not think about all this. I was always striving to do my work properly, and not to come into collision with any one. Besides, such things did not happen in my work-room. No friendly, no kind word came from our foreman. He was a tyrant of the worst sort, and he must have considered the workers a troop of slaves. No one ventured to complain of him. He was considered the most excellent official in the business, to which he, doubtless, was devoted. He had probably quite forgotten that he had once been a workman in the same factory.

I did not wish to leave my mother, and I wanted to manage so that she need not work any longer. I economised just as much as my comrades, and if I spent a half-penny more one day, I literally went hungry the next. I recognised already that I could lay up no fortune for myself; but I wanted to care for my mother, and to have a small sum for necessities, in order to keep her out of the hospital in case of illness, as she had a great dislike to it. Like the other girls, I considered myself lucky to be in this factory, and I anxiously avoided everything which might cause me to be blamed.

"A good master"—that was the general

opinion of my employer. We can see from this manufacturer how profitable is the sweating of human labour. He who really did more for his workers than most employers, he who continued to pay his workers their wages for weeks if they were ill; he who in case of death made a present of considerable sums of money to the survivors; and who scarcely ever refused a request, if any one turned to him in trouble— he had, nevertheless, become rich by the productive labour of the men and women working in his factory.

I will now relate how in spite of all this I became a Social Democrat in this factory. For the time being I no longer considered myself poor. I enjoyed our splendid Sunday dinner, thinking it fit for a royal feast. We bought meat for fivepence, and I cooked it. Later, when my wages were higher, it became "still" better, and I also had a glass of sweet wine to drink.

Only one thing was wanting to make me perfectly contented—all my comrades had been confirmed. They would talk of how splendidly it had gone off, and what presents they had received from their godmothers. But I had not been confirmed, as my mother was too proud to beg any one to be my godmother, and she herself could not afford the white dress and the other things which went with it, however much she would have wished to do so; and I had always been obliged to abandon all thought of it. When it was announced in the papers that on the day of confirmation a godfather or godmother was to be found for a poor child, my mother advised me to try my luck and stand by the church, or else I must wait until I had earned enough to be able to buy everything for myself.

When I was sixteen, and a man first spoke to me of marriage, I answered in all seriousness: "Why I am not yet confirmed." According to my view, a true Catholic must first receive this sacrament before she could think of marriage. I was now seventeen, and did not want to wait any longer. A fellow-worker who was engaged to a young man in better circumstances wished to be my godmother.

At a shop where I could pay by instalments I bought a pretty, light dress, elegant shoes, a silk sunshade, pretty gloves, and, crowning all, a hat trimmed with flowers. Those were splendid things! In addition came the drive in an open carriage, the ceremony in the church with the bishop's laying on of hands, then an excursion, a prayer-book, and some useful presents. Now, for the first time, I seemed to myself quite grown up.

My mother no longer went out to work.

She earned something at home, and looked after the household matters. We had taken a room with two windows, and my youngest brother lived with us again, but without his friend. When I read on Sundays, I could sit by a window that, certainly, only looked into a narrow courtyard; but yet I was very happy. I now read better books, also the classics. Lenau's poems made a great impression on me. I learnt *Anna* by heart, then *Clara Hebert* and the *Albigenses*. I was much fascinated by Wieland's *Oberon*, and I learnt Chamisso's *Lion's Bride* by heart. Goethe did not inspire me. I thought him "immoral" and some epigrams I rejected as "licentious." It was only some years later that the *Elective Affinities* made me decide to read more of Goethe. This, the *Iphigenia*, and *The Natural Daughter*, I read most often.

I was also stronger physically and more capable of endurance. I was pale, but which of my comrades was not? In spite of my good health, I could not lose the recollection of my former state of ill-health. Those dark shadows of the past pursued me, and many a a time I suffered from them quite horribly. The most unlikely things made me think I was going to be ill again. The twitching of an eyelid, a flickering before my eyes, appeared

to me as a threatening of the dreaded illness.
I did not recover from the fright the whole
day. I woke at night full of terror, and complained to my mother; she suffered with me.
The neighbours had all kinds of advice to give
—"sympathetic remedies," as all the super-
stitious things which are often used are called.
I was often depressed for a whole week, which
my fellow-workers put down to love troubles.
I never told them the cause of my sadness;
I did not want to talk of it, as I fancied if I
only mentioned my illness, it would be enough
to bring it on.

As I had heard much talk around me of
how all imaginable troubles could be cured
by a pilgrimage, I wanted to try this remedy
also. I meant to pray most devoutly at the
holy shrine for perfect freedom from my
dreaded illness, which I felt was always
threatening me, and for a sign to tell me my
prayer was granted. We went on foot to
the shrine nine miles off. I was imbued
with the most pious sentiments.

There was only one thing which I found it
difficult to resolve to do. It was considered
important to confess and communicate before
approaching the miracle-working image. But
I had always an unconquerable dislike to that.
Still, I made the journey without eating anything, as one may only receive the Host fasting.

When I knelt at the confessional box, I did not know what to say; the priest waited for my confession of sins, but nothing sinful that I had done occurred to me. At last the priest asked me questions, among them some that confused and hurt me. I answered everything with "no," and was dismissed with a light penance. I went through the prayers of expiation, but I did not receive the communion. In spite of all my piety, I could not force myself to believe in the miracle of the Host, although I still believed in God and His Divine Omnipotence and also in the saints and their intercession. But I had always experienced an instinctive feeling of aversion to, and unbelief in, formalities. I prayed all the more reverently before the image of the crucified Jesus, which lay in a niche, as in a grave. There was a terrible crowd praying. All crept on their knees to kiss the spots pierced by nails of the wooden Saviour. I did so too, and pressed my lips to the same spots which had been touched that day by hundreds and hundreds of the sick and the healthy. In the cloisters I gazed at all the wonderful things that had been given to the holy shrine as thank-offerings. Hands of wax, silver, and gold had been offered in great numbers as thanks for the healing of a hand that had been deemed incurable. Crutches, as a remembrance of the cure of a lame leg. Numerous pictures represented the scene of miracles. In one a child fell from a high storey, and through the miraculous intervention of the Holy Virgin, he fell whole and uninjured. In another picture a child was being saved from the flames by Mary, Queen of Heaven—of course not through the intrepidity of the fire brigade man. I could also see pictures where horses that had shied were running over a child, which, again through the aid of the saints, was uninjured. Thank-offerings for salvation from deadly dangers of every kind, thank-offerings for salvation from lingering illness, and thank-offerings for salvation from bankruptcy, and also for the accomplishment of a happy marriage. The fortunate persons had offered rich gifts for all these wonderful deeds; one could read about all the miracles in the dedications.

I cannot say that I was free from doubts. I had myself only too often prayed in vain for help. But I bought also my sacrificial candle, without knowing that if one really wants it to be offered in sacrifice one must stand by it till it is burnt. It was only later that I attained to the knowledge that one candle is sold over and over again, and that not only the makers of candles make a good business out of these offerings, but the church also gains simple and compound interest on them.

The "chief attraction" of the holy shrine is a miraculous image of the "Mother of God." One reaches the image by a flight of steps, which one may only touch creeping on one's knees. One has to say a paternoster on every step—only thus can one obtain the fulfilment of one's desire from the Merciful One. I saw women creeping from step to step, and I did the same. How this image of Mary was adorned! Silver, gold, and pearls—I was overwhelmed, as I had never seen such abundance and splendour. They all sparkled and glittered on her. But we were not allowed to approach this image; she and her precious ornaments were protected by a railing from any touch. We could only gaze and wish at a reverential distance from the wondrous image. I ought in pious worshipping prayer to breathe my wish to this splendid image. No thought must be directed to the outside world. The soul of the person requesting help must be turned utterly towards God and Mary. What wonder that I came home from the shrine with fearful doubts. Had my glances dwelt too much on the glittering ornaments of the image, so that, as I felt, I had not brought the fit amount of reverential feeling?

The pilgrimage was without result—my anguish was not lessened. I wanted to try once more, and we went to another shrine, which was said to have a greater miraculous power. It was farther off, so that one had an opportunity on the way to expiate for more sins. We started at four in the morning of a hot Sunday in July. We had to walk for five hours. We did not allow ourselves a drop of water on the way. I wanted to renounce, to do penance, in order to be worthy of participating in the blessing. We arrived tired, hungry and thirsty, and covered with dust. Thousands of persons assembled during the morning. Not only the church, but the inns, were overflowing with people. The throng at the service in the church where the pilgrims held their procession of flags was so great that there could be no chance of true devotion. It was a continuous coming, going, pushing, and pressing. Then again cries of help, and still greater crowding, as those who had fainted owing to the bad air had to be taken out. Cripples who were dragging themselves along on crutches; other unfortunates who wore shades in front of their half-blind eyes; sick children on their mother's arms; expectant mothers who wanted to pray for a happy delivery; other women who hoped to obtain the promise of children—they were all in this wild pushing, scuffling, and scolding, and later in the overfull restaurants, where there was unrestrained drinking and noise. I was repulsed and sickened, and made no more pilgrimages. I was not shattered in my belief, but I had a secret presentiment that I could have prayed better at home than in surroundings which reminded me more of the crowd at a parish fair than of a house of God.

. . . .

I did not only like to read novels and tales; I had begun, as I have already mentioned, to read the classics and other good books. I also began to take an interest in public events. I was barely fifteen when a state of martial law was proclaimed at Vienna. One of the proclamations, which began, "My dear Count Taffe," was nailed up in the street in which I worked. As far as I remember, it forbade the assembling of several persons. I read this proclamation with the greatest interest, and came to my companions much excited. I cannot now say what kind of mood overcame me; but I know very well that I mounted on our work-table and made a speech to my "brothers and sisters," in which I made known the proclamation of martial law. I did not really understand anything of the matter; I had no one to talk with about it, and I was, moreover, not democratically inclined. I was full of enthusiasm then for emperors, and kings and highly placed personages played no small part in my fancies. But everything political interested me vividly. On Sundays I very often paid a visit to an old man, an acquaintance of my mother, because he would tell me of wars and historical occurrences. The Mexican imperial drama of the Austrian Archduke Maximilian was discussed again and again.

Even whilst I was an apprentice, I often went without food to be able to buy a newspaper. It was not the news that interested me, but the political leading articles. Now that I had a fixed wage, I bought myself a paper that came out three times a week. It was a strict Catholic paper, that criticised very adversely the workers' movement, which was attracting notice. Its aim was to educate in a patriotic and religious direction. Two points of view struggled for supremacy in me. I took the warmest interest in the events that occurred in the royal families, and was much better informed on the deeds of archdukes and the surroundings of princesses than on the things which concerned my nearest neighbours. I mourned with Spain for Alphonso XII., and I treasured as though it had been a relic the picture which came with my newspaper of Marie Christina as she showed herself to her subjects with her infant in her arms. For the sake of Alexander of Battenberg I desired war and defeat for Russia, and the Bulgarian Prince was to be found for a long time in my picture gallery. I took the death of the Crown Prince of Austria so much to heart that I wept a whole day. But not only the fate of dynasties affected me, political events held me in suspense. The consideration in my paper of the possibility of a war with Russia roused my patriotic enthusiasm. I saw my brother already returning from the battlefield covered with glory, and I would have much liked to see myself in the *rôle* of the " Heroine of Worth," of whom I had read in a novel, and whom William had distinguished with the " Iron Cross."

I read, besides, the histories of the French and Viennese revolutions, which were lent me by the father of one of my companions. I could not for a long time understand and interpret them completely. Indeed, when a particularly strong anti-Semitic feeling was noticeable in political life, I sympathised with it for a time. A broad sheet, " How Israel attained to power and to the sovereignty over all the nations of the earth," fascinated me. There I acquired (in addition to the many atrocious deeds which were wrongly ascribed to the people of Israel) a knowledge of the fabled human sacrifice in their ritual. I read further that the Jews would insult "the daughters of the Christians" to spare their own wives and daughters. This assertion influenced me most. I also wanted to contribute towards keeping in check the Jewish attacks; and I resolved to withdraw my custom from the Jewish shops where I had hitherto bought my clothes. I persuaded my companions to do the same.

About this time an Anarchist group was active. Some mysterious murders which had taken place were ascribed to the Anarchists, and the police made use of them to oppress the rising workmen's movement. I followed it all with burning interest. None of those details for the sake of which people say women read the papers appealed to me. I scarcely glanced at them. I followed the trials of the Anarchists with passionate sympathy. I read all the speeches, and because, as always happens, Social Democrats, whom the authorities really wanted to attack, were among the accused, I learnt to know their views. I became full of enthusiasm. Every single Social Democrat whom I learnt to know in the papers seemed to me a hero. It never occurred to me that I might join in their fight. Everything that I read of them seemed so high and lofty that it would have appeared absurd to me to think that I, an ignorant, unknown, and poor creature might also one day take a part in their struggles.

There was unrest among the workers: unemployment had much increased, whole industries were at a standstill, and the police thought they could suppress the discontent and the growing poverty with underhand tricks. They broke up trade unions and confiscated their funds. That, naturally, increased the feelings of resentment, and demonstrations of protest followed. When these were repeated the military entered the "threatened" streets. Both infantry and cavalry were sent. In the evenings I rushed in the greatest excitement from the factory to the scene of the disturbance. The military did not frighten me; I only left the place when it was "cleared."

Later on we lived with one of my brothers who had married. Friends came to him, among them some intelligent workmen. They read the union paper of their branch, and I was also interested in it. One of these workmen was particularly intelligent, and I liked talking with him best of all. He had taken several journeys, and could talk on many subjects. He was the first Social Democrat whom I learnt to know. He brought me many books, and explained to me the difference between Anarchism and Socialism. I heard from him, also, for the first time, what a republic was, and in spite of my former enthusiasm for royal dynasties, I also declared myself in favour of a republican form of government. I saw everything so near and so clearly, that I actually counted the weeks which must still elapse before the revolution of state and society could take place.

From this workman I received the first Social Democratic party organ. He did not buy it regularly, but only when he came upon it accidentally, as, alas! so many do. But I begged him to bring me the paper every week, and became myself a constant subscriber. The theoretical parts I could not at first understand, but I understood, and took hold of, all that was written of the sufferings of the working classes, and I first learnt from it to understand and judge of my own lot. I learnt to see that all that I had suffered was the result not of a divine ordinance, but of an unjust organisation of society. The descriptions of the arbitrary application of the laws against the workers filled me with boundless indignation. The annulment of the law against Socialists in Germany, under which the Social Democrats had suffered so severely, was greeted by me with great joy, although I was outside the party and known by no one. I had not been at any meetings; I did not even know that women could attend their meetings. Besides, it was quite against my ideas to go alone to an inn. I shunned almost every pleasure, every distraction, to avoid companions who did not suit my frame of mind. My mother had always impressed upon me that "a good girl is sought for at home." So I always sat at home busy with a book or needlework, whilst half unconsciously I developed a powerful longing for intercourse with companions who would share my thoughts and feelings.

In the factory I became another woman after my thoughts had somewhat freed themselves from my late melancholy sentimentality. I had formerly held myself aloof so that too much intimacy might not arise between my fellow-workers and myself. At first it was put down to shyness and modesty, then, when I did not alter, to pride. But as I was always pleasant, and never held aloof when it was a question of some help to be given in common to a fellow - worker, they had become accustomed to my character. The workmen also who joked with the girls in the courtyard during the intervals at last let me go my own way. They very often called me proud when I would not share in their diversions and avoided talking with the men. "She thinks, forsooth, that she will get a count" was often said.

Now that I had an object before me and was thoroughly saturated with the thought that every one ought to know what had been made known to me, I gave up my reticence, and told my comrades all that I had read of the workers' movement. Formerly I had often told stories when they had begged me for them. But instead of narrating Ohnet's "Owner of a Foundry," or of the fate of some queen, I now held forth on oppression and exploitation. I told of accumulated wealth in the hands of a few, and introduced as a contrast the shoemakers who had no shoes and the tailors who had no clothes. I read aloud in the intervals the articles in the Social Democratic paper, and explained what Socialism was as far as I understood it. I defended my party passionately when people talked of Anarchists as though they were the same as Socialists. My activity was not un-noticed—the foremen noticed it and spoke of me. But I strove anxiously to give no just occasion for finding fault with me. Formerly, like the others, I had often arrived late; now

I accustomed myself to be punctual. I was painfully conscientious in my work; the conviction had instinctively come to me that if one wished to serve a great cause one must also do one's duty in small things. I should not then have understood exactly how to express it, but actually I was dominated by this point of view. In the intervals when I read aloud the contents of my newspaper and tried to explain them, it often happened that one of the clerks passing by shook his head and said to another clerk: "The girl speaks like a man."

I now fetched my newspaper myself every week. When I entered the sales-room of the Social Democratic party for the first time, I felt as though I were entering a sanctuary. And when I gave my first 2½d. towards the election fund of the German Social Democracy under the name of "Firm Will," I felt myself already a member of the great army of combatants, although I did not yet belong to any union, and, with the exception of my brother's friend, had not yet spoken to any Social Democrat.

As I constantly read in my paper, "Get new subscribers," "Increase the circulation of your paper," I struggled to work in this direction. When I was able to fetch every week not only one paper, but two, then three, and finally ten copies, my feeling of joy was beyond all comparison. My journey for the paper had always something of a festive nature for me. On that day I put on my best dress, as I used to do when I went to church.

Although very little was written about religion in the Social Democratic newspapers, I had become free from all religious ideas. It had not happened all at once, but had come about gradually. I no longer believed in a God nor a future life; but the thought still came to me again and again that there might be a possibility of the truth of it. On the same day on which I had endeavoured to prove to my fellow-workers that the creation of the world in six days was only a fairy tale, that there could not be an Omnipotent God, because, if there were, so many men would not have to suffer such hardships in their lives — on the evening of that day I folded my hands as I lay in bed and raised my eyes to the image of the Madonna, and I again involuntarily thought: "Still, it may perhaps be true." I had told no one that such doubts troubled me. But I made use of the descriptions of Siberia and the horrible events in the fortress of St Petersburg which became known, and which I read about in my paper, to prove to my companions that there could be no God directing the lives of men.

My Social Democratic convictions became stronger, and I had to suffer a good deal in the factory. The foreman, who had exercised his tyrannical power over the whole of our room, was always brutal and ill-tempered. He seemed to me just like a devil. He was the first man whom I really hated, and although many years have passed since I withdrew from the sphere of his power, I feel even to-day hatred and resentment when I think of him. When in the course of years many things in the factory became worse, the changes were mainly attributed to him. He could make life in the factory a hell for any man who had incurred his anger, even if he had only tried to defend himself from an unjust accusation. I had hitherto never given him cause to trouble himself particularly about me. Now that was all changed, as he noticed my influence on my colleagues. It did not please him, and he began to observe me. He began to supervise my work more particularly; where he had formerly contented himself with looking after me once a day or had often given that up, he now came ten times a day. I was not safe for a minute as to whether he would not come and look at my work in order to find fault with it. If I stood up to get a glass of water, he would follow me, and stand still until I had drunk it, in order to follow me back

92

to the table. He followed up every step I took, every movement that I made. One day my employer spoke to me to tell me that the foreman was displeased with me. "Consider," said he, at the end, "that you have to look after an old mother." I was so disconcerted and taken aback that I could not answer immediately. But when I had collected myself, I looked for him and begged him to say why the foreman was dissatisfied with me. I told him that in spite of the constant inspection my work was always in order. The manufacturer—I no longer looked upon him as my benefactor—looked at me for a minute, and then went away saying : "Very well ; work on as you have done hitherto."

.   .   .   .

I had no notion yet of the "Woman Question." There was nothing about it in my newspaper, and now I only read Social Democratic publications. I was held to be an exception, and I looked upon myself as such. I considered the social question, as far as I then understood it, as a man's question just like politics. Only I would have liked to be a man, to have a right to busy myself with politics. I only heard for the first time that Social Democrats wanted to procure for women equal political rights with men when, after the Congress at Hainfield of the Austrian

Social Democratic Labour Party, I read the Social Democratic Programme. But I still did not know how women themselves might share in the work of the party. Then I read one day the following article in the Social Democratic newspaper.

"'Woman in the Nineteenth Century'—this is the name of a great pageant that was held for benevolent objects. The chief object of the original exhibition was the 'Presentation of Women's Industry.' It is of a piece with the complete frivolity, the complete thoughtless audacity, of benevolent people to make the subject of a great pageant out of the sorest point of the whole social organisation—that ulcer which contains in itself and produces the whole misery of present day humanity. 'Woman in the Nineteenth Century'—the slave who in a double meaning is treated as goods for sale, as an object of lust and an object of sweating—the 'Woman of the Nineteenth Century' as the queen of the pageant! The industry of women was represented: we saw, indeed, the dirty women brickmakers admired by the directors of companies; or the lace-makers, with their daily wage of 7½d. for sixteen hours labour, complimented by their sweaters, the employers of the lace industry; or the slaves of the weaving and spinning industries, and the exploiters probably made an attempt to make clear to them the advantages of night-work; or the poor women who stand in the nail factory with hands grown horny and burnt — all of them trampled on, sweated, kept in drudgery, driven to death. Or has the noble management perhaps represented the governesses, the educated domestic slaves, as servants in all the lower grades are uneducated slaves, both subject to the unbridled ill-temper, the undisguised scorn, of these benevolent folk. And how was the industry of 'Woman in the Nineteenth Century,' which is called prostitution, represented to them, the prostitution 'sanctified by legal marriage,' and the prostitution of the street. If the whole spectacle had not been a hypocritical lie, a diabolical self-deception, had a single ray of the naked truth penetrated into the glittering hall, then, indeed, the picture of 'Woman in the Nineteenth Century' would have sufficed to rouse the management from their infatuation, to frighten them away in shame and horror. But they are blind, and where they are not blind, they hug their self-deception. How could they live without this self-created blindness?"

I read that in the Social Democratic paper, in *my* newspaper, as I called it in joyful pride, and its effect on me was indescribable. I did not sleep—it was as though scales had fallen from my eyes, and I pondered over what I had read. My state of excitement continued, and everything in me spurred me on to action. I could not possibly keep what I had read to myself—the words came to my lips in due form when I wanted to speak. I mounted a chair at home, and held forth as I would have done if I had to speak at a meeting. I was called a "born orator." A friend of my brother's brought me books from the library of the trade union of which he was a member. How I envied all who could be active. "If I were only a man," I kept repeating. I did not then know that I, though only a girl, could do anything in the Socialist movement or in political life. I never heard nor read of women in meetings, and besides, all the exhortations in "my paper" were directed towards workmen and men. When the Socialist Congress at Paris resolved to cease work for one day as a demonstration for the eight hours' day, I stood apart and could do nothing for "the cause." What I told my colleagues, my help in circulating the paper, seemed to me so paltry and insignificant as to offer me no consolation. I learned later to recognise of what priceless worth such activity is in spreading Socialism.

I received many books from the library of the trade union which required earnest thought. I read the *Neue Zeit* (*Modern Times*), and I gleaned something from all the annual publications in the library. But I wanted to educate myself thoroughly, and I had also books brought me that were not Socialist. I worked through nine volumes of the "History of the World," and I also wanted to study the "Book of Discoveries." But all my endeavours were useless, I could not force myself to like this dry literature, only the part about cork interested me because it was connected with my trade.

Friedrich Engel's "The Position of the Working Classes in England" impressed me deeply and strengthened my revolutionary sentiments. A little pamphlet of Lafargue's, "The Right to Idleness," pleased me extremely, and, when I began to speak at meetings, it furnished me with subject matter. I felt great enthusiasm for Ferdinand Lassalle. I read again and again "Science and the Workers," and then "Holidays, the Press, and the Workers" in order to thoroughly understand them. Liebknecht's speech also, which appeared as a pamphlet, called "Knowledge is Power," belonged to the first Socialist writings which influenced me. I learnt by heart a great number of revolutionary poems of Freedom.

Although I busied myself so much with

Socialism I had never as yet been to any meeting; but I followed all accounts of them with burning interest, and knew the names of all the speakers. But at last I made up my mind to be present at a meeting. When one happened to be held on a Sunday at which the best known and most eminent leaders were to speak, my brother went to it with me. It was in December, and dry cold weather had prevailed for weeks. Many people were out of work, and the sky was observed most anxiously to see if snow might not be expected. One often heard it said: "Even God forgets the poor." The long wished for snow had fallen on this Sunday so important for me. We had to work our way through masses of snow. The meeting was in the great hall of a neighbouring workmen's Union. When we arrived men were already standing shoulder to shoulder; they were rubbing their hands and stamping their feet to warm themselves. My heart beat, and I felt how my face glowed as we pressed through the crowd to get near the speaker's platform. I was the only woman in the meeting, and all faces were turned in astonishment towards me as we passed through. I could only see the speaker dimly, as he was hidden in a cloud of tobacco and cigar smoke. He spoke on the "Capitalist Mode of Production."

And here were new revelations to me. I

heard clearly and convincingly expressed that which I had instinctively felt but had never been able to think out. The speaker began with a reference to the fall of snow, and from it explained what was perverted and foolish in the present order of society. What in a sensible state of society would be looked upon as a natural incident and a hindrance to commerce is to-day esteemed a piece of good fortune, by means of which some hundreds of men are preserved from starvation, men who have no work, not because they will not work, but because through a senseless organisation of society and our short-sighted legislation other men must work so long that they die of exhaustion.

This introduction was fixed in my memory, and my mind elaborated it. I went to a second meeting on Christmas Day at which two women were present beside myself. The speaker dealt with the " Contrasts of Classes." He spoke well, effectively, fluently. I heard illustrated the sorrowful history of my own Christmas festivities and the deprivations of the poor contrasted with the superfluities of the rich. Everything urged me to exclaim: " I know that too, I can also tell of such things." But I did not yet venture on a word, I had not even the courage to applaud. I considered it unwomanly and only right for men. Besides, they only talked of men at the meetings. None of the speakers addressed the women, who certainly were only present in very small numbers. It all appeared to be about the suffering and misery of men. I perceived with sorrow that no one spoke about working women, that no one turned to summon them to the fight.

The third meeting that I attended, and which I mention on account of its character, was an election meeting. The police allowed no women at these meetings, and yet I wanted so much to be present. My entreaties prevailed on the organisers to let me in; but I was obliged to stand quite at the back in a corner. For the first time I heard militarism discussed from the Socialist standpoint. And again some of my earlier ideals were shattered. Until now I had looked on militarism as something unavoidable and indispensable. The fact that my brother had worn the " Emperor's coat" had filled me with pride, and he who had not fulfilled this particular duty would not have seemed to me to be a true man. When in my girlish dreams I had pictured the man who would be my husband, military fitness was one of the qualities which he must possess. And now even this ideal was taken away. Militarism was described as an oppression of the people, and I was obliged to agree with this.

War was the massacre of men, not for the defence of the frontier of one's country against a wicked, savage enemy, but in the interests of dynasties, dictated by greed of land or contrived by diplomatic intrigues.

All that I heard appeared to me so natural that I was only astonished because so few men understood these things.

A new world was opened to me in these meetings, and I longed with all my heart and mind to take an active part in it. I wanted to join in the helping and fighting, and did not yet know how I could do so. But under all these influences I was becoming quite another being. People who understood nothing of my political ideals, or who would not understand anything of them, appeared to me simply as enemies. But I wanted to convert, and to discuss politics. I began to go with my brothers and their wives to parties which I had formerly avoided.

I had been called proud and haughty, and had been urged not to lead a convent life but to enjoy my youth. If I went sometimes, I seemed to myself to be making a sacrifice. Now I went willingly. I wanted to have an opportunity of talking about Social Democracy, and was of opinion that one could talk about politics better with men than with women.

I only learnt later how much I had

over-estimated the political knowledge of men. I wanted to collect for the election fund. When I discussed this at a merry party, one man, a tradesman, said: "For the election fund?[1] Who is he? Oh, I know the ostler who met with an accident." And I, a young girl, with no political rights, was obliged to tell the men deemed worthy of a vote what the election fund was, and why we ought to collect for it. They all wondered where I had acquired my "smartness," and who had taught it me. I collected in the factory also. At first only among the fellow-workers I knew best, but the circle was always widening.

Then came the propaganda for the labour holiday on the 1st of May. This brought me into a state of feverish excitement. I wanted to work for it, and sought for companions who thought as I did. I had noticed among the workers one who wore a broad hat. I hoped from it that he might be a Social Democrat. I watched for an opportunity to speak to him, and did things I had never done before. The workmen washed their hands at the end of the day's work in the courtyard. Many girls also went in. I had never done so to avoid being obliged to hear the talk which was distasteful to me. But now I mixed with them and succeeded

[1] "Election fund" in German is one word, and with "the" before it might be taken for "our friend, election-fund."

in speaking to the owner of the broad hat. I was not deceived. He was an earnest, intelligent workman, and a member of the trade union. How glad I was to know I had some one of my opinions in the factory. If he worked among the men and I among the women, we must succeed in getting a Labour holiday on the 1st of May.

And yet we did not succeed. The workers were too dependent on the manufacturer and were unable to understand how they could undertake anything on their own initiative. Dismissal was threatened to all who did not come to work on 1st May. Even on the last of April I was endeavouring to urge the women in my room to a common demonstration for the Labour holiday on 1st May. I proposed that when the master appeared all should stand up and I would lay our views before him. The standing up altogether would make known our solidarity. Many quite agreed with me; but the old woman who had worked for decades in the factory considered that we ought not to do this to the "master." And so all kept their seats when he came. Then I wanted to beg for myself to be set free; but in the evening we were told: "Who does not work on 1st May, can remain away till Monday." That frightened me. I was a poor girl, 1st May fell on a

Thursday: could I lose half a week's pay? Finally I should not have shrunk from it, but I was afraid of being dismissed altogether; and where could I get such good work? And what would become of my poor mother, if I were out of work for a long time? The whole of my sorrowful past rose up before me and I gave way. I gave way, but with clenched fists and angry feelings.

On 1st May, when I went to the factory in my Sunday dress, I saw thousands of men decorated with symbols of May hastening to the meeting. My brother and his friend belonged to the fortunate ones who kept holiday. I do not know what pain I can compare with that which did not leave me all that day. I was constantly expecting that the Social Democrats would come to fetch us by force out of the factory. I rejoiced at the idea, the others were frightened. The wooden shutters before the windows were not taken down nor opened the whole day lest the window should be broken with stones. At the next payment of wages every man and woman received a printed form on which was to be read: " In recognition of fidelity to duty on the part of my staff on 1st May every man shall receive two florins and every woman one." I took my florin which I would have much preferred to have thrown down at my employer's feet—to the office of the fund for those punished for keeping the 1st of May.

On the next May Day I also kept holiday. I did not rest a day without carrying on propaganda for it. And, as after many years I feel with satisfaction, I adopted good tactics. Among my companions were some who were related to master workmen, and who therefore took a special position. I won these for May Day. I inspired them with the aims for which the Labour Day stood, and they allowed themselves to be chosen for the deputation which had to lay before our employer the request to be allowed the workers' holiday. It was a little revolution. Wives, daughters, sisters of master workmen for May Day! My friend on the men's side had done his share nobly, and we received the workers' holiday free on condition that we had to make up the loss of wages to all those who did not wish to join in the holiday. We rifled our money boxes in which we had put our savings for Christmas, as three of our companions were found who were not ashamed to let us pay them for their holiday.

Shortly afterwards I made my first public speech. It was on a Sunday morning at a branch meeting. I told no one where I was going, and as I often went alone on a Sunday morning to visit a gallery or a museum my departure created no sensation. The meeting was attended by three hundred men and nine women, as I learnt later from the branch paper. As women's work was beginning to play an important part in this branch, and the men were already feeling the effect of the supply of cheaper women workers, at this meeting the meaning of trade organisation was to be discussed. There had been a special endeavour to make the meeting known to working women and although hundreds worked in a single factory only nine women had come. When the summoner of the meeting announced this and the speaker referred to it, I felt great shame at the indifference of my companions of my own sex. I took all the expressions as personal to myself and felt myself attacked by the speakers. The speaker described the conditions of women's labour and showed that the holding back, the absence of wants, and the contentedness of women workers were crimes which drew all other evils after them in their train. He also spoke generally on the woman question, and I heard for the first time from him of August Bebel's book, " Woman and Socialism."

When the speaker had finished the chairman announced that those present should express their opinions on this important question. I had the feeling that I must speak. I fancied that all eyes were directed towards me, that all were wanting to hear what I could say in defence of my sex. I lifted my hand and requested permission to speak. They cried "Bravo" before I opened my mouth; merely from the fact that a working woman wanted to speak. As I mounted my steps to the platform my eyes swam and my throat was parched—I felt as though I were choking. But I conquered my excitement and made my first speech. I spoke of the sufferings, the sweating, and the mental poverty of working women. I laid special emphasis on the last, for it seemed to me the foundation of all the other backwardness and harmful characteristics of working women. I spoke of all that I had experienced and had observed among my fellow workers. I demanded enlightenment, culture, and knowledge for my sex, and I begged the men to help us to them.

The applause in the meeting was boundless; they surrounded me and wanted to know who I was; they took me at first for a member of the Branch, and requested me to write an article addressed to working women for the Union paper on the lines of my speech.

That was certainly an awkward task. I had only been to school for three years, I had no notion of spelling nor of composition, and my writing was like that of a child as I had never had the opportunity of practising it. Yet I promised to try to get the article written.

I felt as though I were in an ecstasy of delight as I went home. An unspeakable feeling of happiness inspired me, it seemed to me as though I had conquered the world. No sleep visited my eyes that night. I wrote the article for the Union paper. It was short, and not well expressed, and ran as follows :—

"On the Position of Women occupied as Workers in Factories

"Working Women! Have you ever once considered your position? Do you not all suffer from the brutality and sweating of your so-called masters? Many slaves for wages, work from early morning till late at night, whilst thousands of their sisters, out of work, besiege the doors of factories and workshops because it is not possible for them to obtain work to protect them from hunger and to procure necessary clothing for their bodies. But how far does the wage itself suffice for such long, continuous work?

"Is it possible for an unmarried working

woman to lead a life fit for a human being?
And first of all the married working woman?
Is it possible for her in spite of strenuous work
to care properly for her children? Must she
not hunger and starve in order to procure
what is absolutely necessary for them? That
is the position of the women workers, and if
we look on idly it will never be improved; on
the contrary, we shall continually be more
trodden down and trampled upon.

"Working Women! Show that you are
not quite depraved and mentally stunted.
Rise and recognise that men and women
workers must join hands in a common bond
of union. Do not close your ears to the cry
which goes out to you. Stand by the organisation which will also train women for the social
and political struggle.

"Visit meetings, read workmen's papers,
become workers conscious of the aims and
various divisions of the Social Democratic
party."

Here I must mention one circumstance that
was fortunate for me. I mentioned in one
place that my eldest brother had gone on the
tramp for work after our father's death. We
did not hear of him for many years and later
had only met for a short time. My brother
had become a Social Democrat, and was an
enthusiastic member of the party long before
I made my first speech. We had heard a
rumour of it, it had been told us that he had

such curious views that he looked on all men as his brothers—he was a Socialist. It appeared to me romantic, then I myself developed his mode of thought. But our mother blamed all that she heard of his opinions, never dreaming that under her eyes her daughter had grown into a belief in the same ideas.

At some worker's meeting at which I was present I met my eldest brother, and I was delighted to possess a fellow believer in a member of my family. Through him I now learnt to know many persons whom I had only hitherto admired at a distance.

.   .   .   .

One day I was sent for to my "master's" office. This was the first time it had happened during the seven years I had worked in the factory. My heart beat indeed as I walked towards the office followed by the curious looks of my colleagues. The manufacturer awaited me with the Social Democratic paper in his hand. My name, with others, was attached to an appeal to collect for the press funds for starting a Social Democratic paper for women. My employer addressed me as " Miss ——," which was not his custom in talking to the other workers, and asked whether I knew the paper and had signed the appeal. On receiving my answer in the affirmative he spoke to this effect: " I can give you no orders as to how you spend your free time; but I beg this one thing of you: Abandon any agitation for these objects in my factory. I likewise forbid any meeting for the support of your aims. I will have peace and quiet in my house." Finally he added: "I will give you one warning on your way; you are young and cannot judge of what you are doing but observe that politics is a thankless business."

Although I resolved to take to heart the words of the manufacturer and not to carry on an agitation in the factory, I could not avoid doing so. For many things had become worse, many favourable conditions had been abolished. In some factories, owing to the influence of the May Day celebrations, they were only working ten hours, but we still always worked eleven. We were to be fined if we had ventured to join in the 1st of May celebrations. In that my employer did not differ from so many other manufacturers. He felt himself the master and bread-giver, and the workmen ought to be grateful for his kindness and favour. Because we had ventured for once to carry through a course of action of which he disapproved, we must be punished. It was only when I was no longer in the factory that the working day was shortened by an hour, but the written pledge was exacted from all men and women workers that they would have nothing to do with me and the Socialist agitation.

I saw many things now with other eyes than formerly. A number of girls were working in the factory who had not yet reached the age prescribed by law. If the inspector's visit were expected—and it was always known in some astonishing manner when the visit was to be expected — it was enjoined on those children that in case they were asked their age, they were to say they were already fourteen. Formerly, like the others, I had thought "our good employer does these unpleasant things because he is sorry for the poor." Since I had read Engel's "Position of the Working Classes in England" I judged differently. I had now other ideas about child labour, and when I had learnt to observe objectively my horrible childhood in the workshops of the middlewoman and in the factories, I drew other conclusions. Besides I saw that just those working women who had entered the factories as children were the most Conservative and the most impervious to all appeals for solidarity. They considered themselves as part of the factory without recognising how small a share of the wealth created by it came to them. They were the most humble and the most cringing of all the workers, and only had a feeling of gratitude to their good master who had given them bread all their lives. They looked with hatred and horror on my actions and on those of my companions who thought as I did. What wonder that I now liked best to draw the attention of the factory inspector to the employment of children of thirteen years of age, and how everything was cleaned and polished when the official was expected. A frenzy of cleanliness existed whilst at other times dust and dirt were allowed to accumulate peacefully for weeks.

My critical observations were directed also to other things. We belonged now to a sick fund, and our representative on the governing body had always up to now been nominated by the manufacturer in the name of the employees. I now knew that we had the right to choose him. In conjunction with the workmen whom I have already mentioned as sharing my opinions, I made this right a reality. And it actually came to a meeting in the factory courtyard, which passed without any further consequences. Great strikes came to pass, thousands of fathers of families had to be supported in order to save them, their wives and children from starvation. The organisations had no longer any funds, the workmen's press asked for collections, and I also considered it my duty to ask for contributions from my fellow-workers—men and women. I was successful with most. But the manufacturer heard of the collections. I appeared to him to be troublesome, for one day he again spoke to me. He asked me to bring him some writing of my own, he wanted to make use of me elsewhere. I was anxious and frightened when I thought of my bad spelling and ugly writing. I was very little troubled about *what* I had written. I was just then reading Goethe's Poems and I copied a stanza from *Prometheus* which pleased me extremely :

> " When I was a child
> And knew not whence I came
> Nor whither I was going,
> I turned my wandering eye
> Towards the sun as though beyond it
> Was an ear to hear my plaint,
> A heart like mine
> To pity the oppressed."

I was directed the next day to take the place of a sick clerk. A few years ago I should have been exceedingly delighted at this request. How I should have rejoiced at not being obliged to continue to be a factory hand ! It would have appeared to me to be quite easy to overcome all difficulties. Now I had become more sensitive. It oppressed me to occupy a place for which all preliminary knowledge was wanting in me.

I certainly understood mental arithmetic, but I had no idea how to calculate with a pencil. The little multiplication and division that I had learnt in the elementary school was long forgotten. If, however, I had felt a strong inclination for this post, I would not have been afraid of learning, but the new position took me away from my colleagues. I could no longer carry on a propaganda. Since my first speech I was in much request for meetings. Every Sunday, and often several times in the week, there were meetings at which I had to speak. But in the office I had to work an hour later in the evenings and it was then too late to attend meetings. On the whole my hours of work were shorter, and I did not have to go till 8 in the morning, and had two hours free at noon so that I could go home, and I at once received a florin more a week. But it gave me no satisfaction. Only political activity could content me. When the sick clerk was well I went back to the factory room, which I much preferred to the post in the office, for which I had no aptitude, and where there was no one to tell me how to pick up what I had forgotten or not learnt.

I had become an object of general attention. My speeches were written about in the papers, the police served me with notices to learn about the charges which I had raised at meetings over cases of sweating of working women and of ill treatment of domestic servants. The agitation engrossed me more and more. I had become a member of the managing committee of an organisation of working women, and had to take part in many meetings. I was quite engrossed with my public work and was ready for any sacrifice. I had often to give up my dinner to pay for the fee for opening the gates after hours when I came home late in the evening. Then I bought for three farthings some soup for dinner and bread. But it would not have done for my mother to know that my public work cost money. So I had actually secretly to go without something in order to deceive her, for had she known that it cost money when I made a speech at a meeting it would have been worse for me.

The books which I wanted to study I borrowed from the library of the Union. I spoke on " The Press and Literature," on the " Aims and Use of Organisation," but most willingly on the " Position of Working Women." Then I could speak on what I knew from my own experience. My sufferings were also the sufferings of others. As I developed my work under such difficult conditions people felt all the more the truth of what I said. When I urged others to overcome all difficulties, I used no empty phrases, because I myself was constantly struggling against just such great obstacles, against material poverty, and against the mental pain I had to endure through my mother. Even then malicious speeches were made on the luxuries in the lives of Social Democrats. My mother heard of them, and as she was told that I was called a leader in the papers, my situation became worse still. Why was not her daughter, who was so brilliant, not also paid? So she asked. I had to take refuge in many necessary fibs in order to make her feel more favourably. But, at the same time, I suffered from poor nourishment and the double work, to work eleven hours in the factory and to attend committees and meetings two or three times a week, which in those stormy times always ended at a late hour. It was worst of all once on a Saturday evening when I had to give an address on the "Woman Question" in a very distant district and only reached home at midnight. I had to start again at 5 in the morning to reach a station nearly three miles off to make a three hours' journey to a meeting in the country. Again I only reached home at midnight, and had to walk for an hour without having eaten one good meal in the day. At home I dared not let anything be noticed of it; with painfully repressed tears of anguish I had to represent things to my mother as though I had earned something by my journey. If my comrades in the country had had a suspicion of how it was with me, they would certainly not have allowed me to suffer such privations. But I myself could give nothing away, and I would not receive anything from others. Perhaps this point of view may seem exaggerated to many, but it was only the consequence of my former mode of looking at things. The next day, tired and without proper nourishment, I had to be at the factory at 7 A.M. When I had worked for about an hour a sudden giddiness attacked me, and I fell from my chair unconscious. I was taken home and examined by a doctor, who again recommended good food, fresh air, and plenty of sleep. But I had only the one wish, to be well again, and to be able to learn enough to be capable of performing my duties. Since I had become ill again I lived in a constant state of anxiety. In the midst of a speech my eyes swam and I fancied I should lose consciousness, and I used superhuman energy in order to conquer my fear.

When I next went into the country I succeeded in persuading my mother to accompany me. If I had her beside me, my anxiety tormented me less, I felt more secure. For the first time she heard me speak at a meeting to hundreds of people. She heard the applause which was accorded to me, and heard with what appreciation earnest men spoke of me to her. She cried—not at what I said as many did—but from pity because she had the impression that speaking so loudly for so long would hurt my health. She was not able to take in the meaning of my words. She, who could not read a line and whose German vocabulary, in consequence of her Bohemian parentage, was not very rich, could not understand my expressions at all. It has always grieved me that I have found no understanding sympathy in the mother I loved so much.

In the factory I felt more and more uncomfortable. On all lips the question was shaping itself: "How long still?" The State authorities began to give me more of their attention. Detectives came to our house to enquire about me. My mother, who heard of it, was very uneasy. I myself was anxious on her account. What would become of her if they imprisoned me? But still I could not give up my work. I was too thoroughly permeated with, and inspired by, Socialist aims. Once a paper was sent to me at the factory, in which it was stated that the State authorities had ordered my arrest. "What will my mother say?" was my first thought. But the paper had exaggerated. Only an examination was initiated, which, later, was discontinued.

When I shortly after was chosen to devote all my time to the organisation among working women, and to help to work at a newspaper for working women, I received a testimonial from the manufacturer that praised my diligence and extraordinary application. He handed it to me with the words: "I wish you may find as much appreciation in your new sphere of work."

I was now endlessly happy. I had a sphere of work which satisfied all my longings but which I had considered quite unattainable for myself. It was to me the Promised Land. My mother had no pleasure in my altered mode of life. She would have preferred me to have remained in the factory, and then to have married. The old woman, who looked back on a long series of sufferings and deprivations, who under the most terrible conditions had borne a child every two years and had then fed it at the breast for sixteen or eighteen months to be saved longer from another confinement, this woman, crippled and prematurely bent from hard work, could picture no other lot for her daughter than a good marriage. To marry her daughter well was her thought and aspiration, and I had much to go through when I was still working in the factory, if I refused a marriage, the only object of which was to lighten my lot and free me from the factory. She looked on marriage and children as the destiny of a woman. However much at first she was flattered by the praise of me that she heard, to just the same degree later was she displeased when she perceived that I wanted to devote myself to public work. The more busy I was as a speaker, the more unhappy she became.

Although she was not exactly religious—life had been too hard to her for that—still she clung very much to appearances. My views, which were now quite adverse to religion, roused her displeasure, and she repeated everything she heard from ignorant or malicious persons about Social Democrats. She continually hurt and mortified me by these wicked speeches about the party to which I had attached myself. As through my ever increasing work I often came home at a later hour in the evening than in her eyes a properly brought up girl should do, she began to be ashamed of me. If I came home tired and overworked, she waited for me to make a scene and abuse me. If I came home with a feeling of contentment, because I had done useful work elsewhere, this joy was embittered by the scorn which I had to expect from her. I often lay in bed for hours weeping, weeping bitter tears because Fate was so hard on me.

Now that I had a career that inspired me, that gave me happiness and joy, I had to suffer because my mother was too old to sympathise with me.

But the thought of leaving her never occurred to me. We had borne so much sorrow together, how should she not be with me now that many dark shadows had vanished from me? For now that my life was so full I began to loose more and more the sad thoughts of the past. I felt healthy and strong enough to bear the heaviest labours of my self-chosen work. Only my mother's dislike of it weighed ever more heavily on me. She hindered my development and I had to drag myself along as if in any heavy fetters.

But I will gratefully mention one attempt which was made to bring my mother round and reconcile her to her work.

Friedrich Engels was travelling over the Continent and I learnt to know him. He possessed a winning kindliness of manner, so that I did not feel I was meeting one of the great men of the International party. As then only few women were working for the party, and as the leaders considered the help of women useful, Friedrich Engels interested himself even in my development. When he talked with me I told him of what was nearest my heart—of my mother. He wanted to help me and to lighten my path in life. He, with August Bebel, came to me in my modest suburban home. They wanted to make the old lady understand that she ought to be proud of her daughter. But my mother, who could neither read nor write, and who had never understood anything of politics, could not understand the good intentions of the two leaders. Both were famous throughout Europe, their revolutionary writings and speeches had aroused the authorities all over the world; but they met the poor old woman without making any impression on her, she did not even know their names.

When we were alone again, she said disdainfully: "So you bring old men here." In her eyes it was always a question of a wooer for me with every man who came, and as it was her most earnest longing to see me married, every one was looked on in that aspect. Our two visitors, one of whom was an old man whilst the other could have been my father, did not appear to her to be suitable as a husband for her young daughter.

I would willingly have fulfilled my mother's wish to marry; but I could not give up my ideals merely to be cared for and to be able to lead a life free from poverty. I had become too independent in my way of thinking. I was too deeply penetrated by the conviction that Socialism was not only necessary but that it would bring about the salvation of the world. My belief in it had become unalterable, and when I thought of marriage I dreamed of a husband who would share my ideals. From him I expected not only the happiness that comes to like-minded persons striving towards the same goal, but also help in my own development. This happiness was granted to me. I obtained a man for a husband who shared my opinions and whose character attained the ideal of which I had dreamed. There was no greater pleasure to him than to witness my enthusiasm for the party for which long before I knew of him he had sacrificed and suffered. He shared all my sorrows and cares, he lightened my path whenever he could. He gave up many personal comforts to render possible my propaganda work among working women. Women had no more sympathetic friend than he was, and he often told me how it had grieved him when he saw women, some of them weak, tender creatures, slipping about, up to their knees in dirt, cleaning the pavements. In bitter words, he spoke of the men who drank or gambled away half their week's wage, whilst wife and children drudged at home.

He honoured the woman worker, not only the woman earning wages but also the slave to work, the woman busy in her house, and he inveighed against the injustice of considering the work of the latter, often tiring and exhausting, as play. When I went with him from home, having already put our room in order whilst he was sitting with a book or newspaper, he never looked on it as a matter of course but as going beyond my duty.

My mother managed our house, but as in her deeply rooted convictions the woman belonged to her home, she could not help expressing her bitter displeasure at my not keeping exclusively to my own fireside. To avoid vexations I had to devote many hours and many a half day to household work which others could have done just as well. At night I had to make good where I was behind hand in consequence either in my writing or my self-improvement.

My mother had been very much against this marriage. She could not pardon me for having chosen a husband who was old enough to have been my father. But she could but acknowledge the excellence of his character and the worth of his individuality. She esteemed him highly, and later had real sympathy with him. How often the tired, worn-out man would sit for hours trying to make clear to her what a splendid cause was Socialism! He told her of Christ and His work to make it more intelligible to her. She often agreed with him, but the next day she went back to her old opinions. She was too old to understand fresh points of view.

When in the fourth year of our marriage I was expecting our first child I busied myself much with domestic matters, and stepped into my mother's place with the cooking. Now that which she had so desired aroused her jealousy. She considered herself displaced by me, and when my husband spoke gratefully of my work as a housekeeper she sought to disparage my capabilities. It was touching to hear my husband explain to her how honourable it was to her daughter to have learnt without schooling and instruction that which had only with difficulty been taught to others. I suffered very much, from these actions of my mother's, which did not spring from malice but from the disappointment she had experienced in me. She had desired my marriage so very much, and she had expected through it that I should become like other women, and make an end to my work at meetings.

Now I was married, but I was not less

active than before, and my husband lived for the same work. When we came home at night she awaited us sitting up in her bed and pouring out doleful complaints. She reproached us both severely. My husband was so full of consideration and so tender-hearted that he never spoke a harsh word to her. But how he suffered from it, and what self-control he exercised!

She scoffed and sneered when my husband encouraged me to have instruction from a teacher because I felt myself so weak in spelling and grammar. But my husband also encouraged me in my desire to learn foreign languages. He was influenced by the thought that with more education and greater know-ledge I should be better able to serve the proletariat.

Later, when we had children, I often thought I should break down under the double burden. Many a time I sat by the writing table with my infant in my arms and wrote articles whilst the household work was still to be done. I had no help in the housework except from my mother. But my mother was over seventy and sickly. If my husband and I had had our will, she would long ago have given up work. But she would not suffer any one to take her place. She was always afraid of seeming not to be wanted, and she clung to her sphere of work for which she was no longer fit. So I had to work day and night. When my child was four months old I was so much weakened that one day, just after I had put it to sleep, I became insensible. I felt desperate at the verdict of the doctor, who said I ought not to nurse the infant any longer. I seemed to myself to be unworthy, and I pitied my child. But all that could have been spared me if I had not had to bear more than a double burden. When the thought tormented me that I could not quite fulfil any of my duties, and at the sight of my child I would willingly have resolved to give up everything else completely during the time it needed me most. Then it was my husband who encouraged me. He represented to me that later, when the child no longer needed my peculiar care, I should be unhappy if now in the conflict between the duties of mother-hood and of my public vocation I withdrew altogether from political work.

When these conflicts recurred with increased force after the birth of our second child, my husband was already conscious that no great length of life would be granted him. He saw that I should have to care for, and bring up, the children alone. Even before the birth of our second child he had felt very ill, and had foreseen his approaching end.

He had often lamented that he had come in my way and had asked me to marry him. He saw clearly how difficult it would be for a woman to work for, and bring up, two children. But even under the difficult conditions under which we lived, he had never attempted to restrain me from fulfilling my duties for the movement. When I had to go away some days to meetings, I often entreated: "Do say for once that you do not want me to leave you alone with the children, then I shall find it easier to draw back." But he answered in his simple goodness: "For my own sake and for that of the children I should wish you to stay here; but as a member of the party, I wish that you should not draw back from performing your duty." When I was away he wrote to me daily about his health and the children's. He did not forget anything that was calculated to make me easy. In spite of the heavy burden of work and the great responsibility he had to bear, he forced himself to save time to look after the children and watch over their health. Therefore I always understand how heavy public work is for a mother, because I know what a sacrifice it entails. What has not my husband gone without to make such work possible for his wife—work which he considered useful to the working classes. But from it I have also experienced how happy and untroubled a marriage can be, if it rests on perfect harmony of thought and feeling, when the husband recognises the capabilites of his wife, and does not only desire that his capabilities shall receive recognition from her.

Alas! our happiness did not last long. It was not even granted us to pass nine years of life together. How willingly would he have lived perhaps to enjoy an easier future with his children. It was not permitted him. I myself had long known that he could only live a short time. Already, in the second year of our marriage, the doctor had drawn my attention to the critical state of his health, and had prepared me for possibly a sudden end. I saw all those years what he suffered, and, frightened to death, I often woke suddenly on hearing him groan, and saw him lose his colour and struggle for breath. In the greatest anguish he would often jump out of bed, tormented with terrible pains in the head. Then, again, cramp in the feet would seize him, or he could not sleep because he had a fearful empty feeling in the head.

Once when I came home from a long propaganda journey which I had undertaken at his express wish, I found him so ill that I immediately fetched the doctor. My husband never again left the sick-bed to which, after much persuading, he now betook himself.

I had learnt to know him as a sick, tired man. I have mentioned how I always put on my pretty clothes when as a factory worker I fetched the Social Democratic paper. There I saw my future husband, always suffering, often with a grey silk handkerchief round his neck. When we had seen one another several times, he told me of his solitary existence; of his cold room, in which he froze, and which no one heated for him; and of the uncomfortable life in inns and coffee-houses, that was so injurious to his sickly body. I should not then have dreamed that I could be his wife. But I learned to esteem him more and more, and felt hearty sympathy for him. His wise prudence and his energetic character impressed me. Without his doing anything to cause it, the wish grew stronger in me to brighten his life and to draw him from his joyless loneliness. He gave me, as I indeed acknowledged, prudent, well-meant advice as to my behaviour in various episodes of my life, and I always found his advice good and useful. It was curious; he was the first man for whom my sympathy increased the more I knew of him. In my most secret thoughts I considered the question whether I could be happy with him, and weeks before he had spoken a word of love to me I considered myself as belonging to him. I have never repented entering into this marriage. It changed me from a precociously serious girl into a joyous woman. Only when I became wholly conscious of the danger in which he always lived, anxiety came again—secret, gnawing anxiety. When I knew from the doctor that any excitement might be fatal to him, I was constantly striving in secret to keep from him anything that might excite him. With what difficulty, and how seldom, I succeeded! As he belonged to those extremely conscientious men who are resolved to do their duty to the utmost and to show no consideration to themselves, none of those round him, myself excepted, had any idea of the need for his sparing himself. But what courage he must have had to discharge the duties laid upon him.

Had we been in good circumstances financially, could he only for once have allowed himself thorough relaxation and rest from the many cares which were laid upon him, he would probably have lived some years longer. But there was no rest, indulgence, and recreation for him, for which his exaggerated conscientiousness concerning the work entrusted to him was partly responsible. So he also did not share the happiness of living to see that for which he was daily ready to sacrifice his life—the growing greatness and power of the working classes.

.   .   .   .

My mother felt for me for the first time. How much she had learnt to prize and love my husband can be shown by her exclamation : " If only I could have died, and he be spared ! " She tried to comfort me, often with the hint that I might have another husband — a younger one.

But I had my children ; and I sought comfort in the thought that perfect happiness comes to no one. And Socialism had given to me so much, had lent my life so much peace, that I had strength to go through much without succumbing. To be inspired to serve a great cause gives so much joy, and lends such high worth to life, that one can bear very much without losing courage. I learnt to acknowledge that in my own experience.

.   .   .   .

When I felt the necessity of writing how I became a Socialist, it was solely with the wish of encouraging those numerous working women who possess hearts full of a longing desire to do something ; but who always draw back again, because they do not trust their own capabilities. Socialism could change and strengthen others, as it did me. The more consciously I became a Socialist, the more free and strong I felt to meet all opponents. My belief in Socialism had become strong as a rock, and I was never tempted for a moment to waver in it.

When, after my marriage, I was once imprisoned on account of a critique on the present institution of marriage, I never for a moment thought of repentance as I sat lonely in my bare cell. On the contrary, when in the twilight I walked up and down my solitary cell, which I could pace with fourteen steps, I meditated on how I could make up for my lost time. I worked at educating myself further in Socialism, and read scientific books, for which I had usually no time. When my husband came to visit me, I could not wait to read the party organ which he secretly slipped into my hands. It was not pleasant in the cell with the peephole, through which the warder could look as often as he pleased. How frightened I was when at six in the morning the warder came with a prisoner to bring water; how it robbed me of sleep if the gas was left burning at night in the cell so that they could see me at any time through the peephole! In the exercise in the courtyard I had to walk ten steps behind the other prisoners so that they might not talk politics with me. And if one woman remained behind to address me and ask the reason of my presence there, how vulgarly and roughly she was abused by the warder!

On my bed I fancied I was lying on stones, and my limbs ached from the hardness; but no thought of repentance came to me. My confidence was deep-rooted that the truth of the saying of George Herwegh's, which so often adorns the walls at workmen's festivals, would be realised by the victorious power of the proletarian struggle for freedom :—

> "What do we desire of the distant future?
> That we may be provided with bread and work;
> That our children may learn in the schools;
> And that our old people may not go begging."

Who really desires to help make Herwegh's words reality must shrink from no difficulty. The goal is wonderfully beautiful; it is so promising that strength can be found to conquer any difficulty in the way. If I have succeeded in helping to this end in my modest work, then I have attained my aim.

Printed at
The Edinburgh Press
9 and 11 Young Street.

CPSIA information can be obtained at www.ICGtesting.com
Printed in the USA
BVOW04s1609070815

412146BV00007B/46/P